ELIZABETH
TAYLOR

ELIZABETH TAYLOR

A BIOGRAPHY IN PHOTOGRAPHS

A JAMES SPADA ASSOCIATES BOOK

BY

CHRISTOPHER NICKENS

HUTCHINSON

London Melbourne Sydney Auckland Johannesburg

ACKNOWLEDGMENTS

For Jim, for reasons too numerous to mention.
And in fond memory of Louise Hartwell.

I am especially grateful to Bill Goulding, whose devotion to
Elizabeth Taylor has resulted in an encyclopedic knowledge about her
life that was invaluable to me. Also extremely helpful were
James Breen, Ernie Vaht, Lou Valentino, George Zeno, Guy Vespoint,
Bob Combs, Michel Parenteau, Jeff Schaffer, and Robert Scott.
A grateful nod also to Stuart Timmons and the staff of the
Academy of Motion Picture Arts and Sciences Library.

For their encouragement, thanks to Jerry Clar, Dan Conlon,
Bruce Mandes, Richard Parker, Vernon Patterson, the Spinner family,
Michael Minor, and Karen Swenson. To Laura Van Wormer and
Kathy Robbins, thanks for taking a chance.

Special gratitude for their patience and understanding must go to
Toni, Gregory Rice, Ken de Bie and Paul O'Driscoll.

A special Thank You is due Thomas Gates for his extensive help
in selecting many of the photographs.

DESIGNED BY KEN de BIE

Hutchinson & Co. (Publishers) Ltd
An imprint of the Hutchinson Publishing Group
17–21 Conway Street, London W1P 6JD

Hutchinson Publishing Group (Australia) Pty Ltd
PO Box 496, 16–22 Church Street, Hawthorne, Melbourne, Victoria 3122
PO Box 151, Broadway, New South Wales 2007

Hutchinson Group (NZ) Ltd
32–34 View Road, PO Box 40–086, Glenfield, Auckland 10

Hutchinson Group (SA) Pty Ltd
PO Box 337, Bergvlei 2012, South Africa

First published in Great Britain 1984
© Spada Publications Inc. 1984

Printed in Great Britain by Jolly & Barber Ltd, Rugby, Warwickshire
and bound by Butler & Tanner Ltd, Frome, Somerset

ISBN 0 09 159101 5

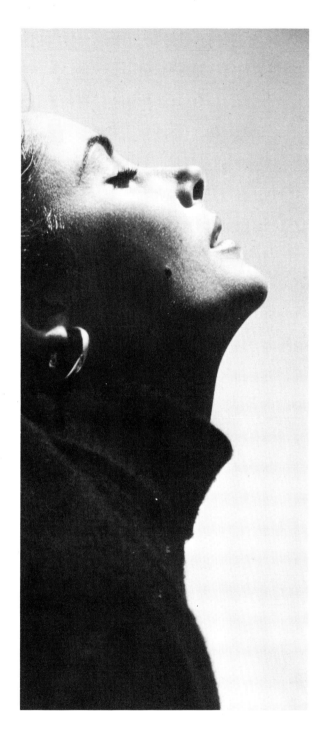

CONTENTS

1
PRINCESS
1932-1950

Elizabeth Taylor's life has often taken on storybook qualities. If her adult years read like romantic fiction, then her childhood can only be described as a fairy tale. Her father Francis was a darkly handsome, sophisticated art dealer, and her mother Sara had enjoyed a brief career as a vivacious, popular stage star. During the Twenties, they toured Europe extensively in search of the fine paintings Francis needed for his growing business. They were an attractive American couple who had no trouble fitting into the finest Continental social circles.

Their carefree travelings came to an end only because Sara discovered she was pregnant. They settled in London, where their son Howard was born in 1929. He was immediately hailed as a baby of rare beauty—"Like a Boticelli angel," his mother said. When his sister came along three years later, it was a surprisingly different story.

Elizabeth Rosemond Taylor was born in London on February 27, 1932. *Rosemond* was in honor of a favored aunt, and *Elizabeth* was the name of both parents' mothers. As a newborn baby, Elizabeth was alarmingly unattractive; her body was covered with a down of black hair. Within a few months, however, she had blossomed into a child of singular beauty. Her disarming looks, combined with the privileged lifestyle her parents were able to give her, set her apart from other children. She was never "spoiled," though, and she paid little attention to the fuss that was usually made over her.

"I had the most idyllic childhood in England," Elizabeth reflected years later, and it was true: she was afforded luxuries and opportunities most little girls in the Depression era seldom dreamed of. She was presented with a horse for her third birthday, and made her stage debut (as an angel in a dance school recital) in front of an audience that included the future Queen Elizabeth.

This charmed period in her life took a dramatic turn when Francis, knowing that England was plunging into war, shipped his family off to California for what was intended as a temporary stay. It was a fateful decision. Beautiful little Elizabeth found herself in the middle of the film-making community, where child stars were still very much in vogue. With the encouragement of her mother, and the skepticism of her father (who joined his family after securing an art gallery in prestigious Beverly Hills), Elizabeth began her movie career at nine years of age.

After only four movies, Elizabeth Taylor became a star when *National Velvet* opened in 1944. Put under contract to Hollywood's biggest studio, she spent her adolescence learning to be a movie star.

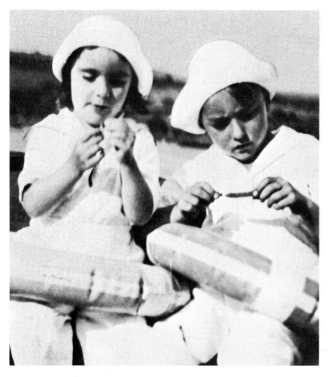

Opposite: Destined to become one of the most photographed women of all time, Elizabeth Taylor seems disinterested as she is presented for one of her earliest portraits by her mother Sara, 1932. Elizabeth's future beauty was not apparent in infancy. In fact, at birth she was something of a horror; her body was covered with black hair, and her eyes were squeezed shut for over a week. Sara admitted that she was afraid she had given birth to the missing link. Within a year's time, however, her daughter's looks had improved considerably. Strangers stopped and gaped at her heart-shaped face, lustrous dark hair and—most of all— her enormous violet eyes, fringed by precociously lengthy lashes.

Above Left: During her fourth summer, Elizabeth plays on the beach with her older brother Howard. By this time, both children were strikingly good-looking. Francis and Sara Taylor often received invitations to swank affairs where the presence of their exquisite children was practically mandatory. Fortunately, neither Elizabeth nor her brother were particularly impressed with the attention they inspired. Sara recalled a typical time with the children during the redecorating of their summer cottage: "Elizabeth and Howard were mainly occupied with getting in our way, smearing themselves from head to foot with paint and stuffing themselves with ginger snaps."

Fearlessly, Elizabeth poses with "Jocko" the chimpanzee at the Regents Park Zoo in London, 1936. The monkey had to be subdued by guards when his fondling of Elizabeth became too enthusiastic. The subject of his affection was unfazed; her remarkable rapport with animals was already becoming evident.

Top Right: A family portrait from the late 1930s in which Francis Taylor is conspicuous by his absence. Always shy, Elizabeth's father was never comfortable in the limelight (he insisted that his wife give up her acting career when they married) and he became a reluctant participant in his daughter's fame.

It was around this time that Elizabeth was first approached to act in movies and, of course, her beauty was an important factor. But it was her singing voice(!) that first intrigued studio talent scouts. At this time, she possessed a sweet, true soprano and was studying with Deanna Durbin's vocal coach. Elizabeth landed an interview at MGM, where studio chief Louis B. Mayer took one look at her and said, "Well. . .what are you waiting for? Sign her up!" Surprisingly, Sara turned down the $1000 a week offer in favor of a contract with Universal, a studio of less prestige. Years later, Sara said that she chose Universal because she felt, wrongly as it turned out, that Elizabeth would receive more personal attention from the smaller studio. She failed to mention that the contract she chose would pay her daughter *double* the MGM salary.

Opposite: In her film debut, Elizabeth is paired with Carl "Alfalfa" Switzer of *Little Rascals* fame. The picture, *There's One Born Every Minute*, was a sophomoric comedy that was so forgettable it was never reviewed in the press. Publicized as a "nine-year-old singer and dancer," Elizabeth made little impact in the only film she made during her 1941 stay at Universal. Years later she recalled, "We played two brats, and as I remember it, all I did was run around and shoot rubber bands at ladies' bottoms."

Following this inauspicious debut, Elizabeth found herself out of a job when the studio dropped her option. At the time, casting director Dan Kelly offered the now infamous explanation of her failure to impress the Universal brass: "The kid has nothing. Her eyes are too old. She doesn't have the face of a kid."

Bottom Right: Before long, Elizabeth was signed by MGM to play Nigel Bruce's granddaughter in *Lassie Come Home*. Auditioning with a floor mop in place of a canine actor, Elizabeth impressed the producer with her looks, manners and prerequisite English accent. Released in 1943, the sentimental family adventure was important to Elizabeth for several reasons; it marked the start of her tumultuous relationship with MGM, the beginning of an enduring friendship with costar Roddy McDowall, and her first reviews. *Variety* called her "a pretty moppet" and *The Hollywood Reporter* prophesized, "Elizabeth Taylor looks like a comer."

A rare portrait from *Jane Eyre*, the 1944 Twentieth Century-Fox release which starred Orson Welles and Joan Fontaine. Elizabeth gave a poignant performance as an abused orphan in the film's early sequences, and she played her first death scene. Although well acted, her role was peripheral to the storyline, and her scenes are often deleted from prints of the moody classic.

Following *Jane Eyre*, Elizabeth played a small role in the Irene Dunne tearjerker *The White Cliffs of Dover* for MGM. Released in 1944, the film reunited Elizabeth with Roddy McDowall, who once again played her "love interest."

Opposite: A costume test for the movie that changed Elizabeth Taylor's life forever: *National Velvet.* Although it starred Mickey Rooney at the height of his popularity, the film turned into a showcase for Elizabeth, who felt she was born to play Velvet Brown, the English girl who, disguised as a boy, jockeys her horse to victory in the Grand National Race. Producer Pandro S. Berman had originally purchased the best-selling Enid Bangold novel as a vehicle for Katharine Hepburn, to be produced at RKO during the 1930s. Consequently, Berman was not initially receptive to Elizabeth's campaign (waged with the considerable aid of her mother) to play Velvet. He felt she was too young, too delicate and at least "three inches too short."

This height discrepancy became a *cause célèbre* for MGM's publicity mill when Elizabeth claimed, after several months, to have grown the required amount in order to do the film. Even after casting her in the role, Berman was skeptical: "Considering Mickey is only titty-high, she really didn't have to grow that much."

Above: With co-stars "Butch" Jenkins and Mickey Rooney astride an obviously fake version of Velvet's horse. The real horse, "Sir Charles," was an unruly beast that became completely charmed by Elizabeth and followed her around the film's locations like a lap dog. Only once was there a problem between horse and actress. Sara recalled her daughter's bravery after the mishap: "The last day of the picture the horse stepped on her foot and injured it badly. But she insisted it didn't hurt and went on working. When she was finished, her foot was so badly swollen we had to slit her jodhpur boot and cut it off. Even when we took her to the hospital, there was not a whimper."

Opposite: Director Clarence Brown had nothing but praise for his spunky *National Velvet* star: "There's something behind her eyes that you can't quite fathom. Something Garbo had. I really hate to call her an actress. She's much too natural for that."

National Velvet was an instant sensation when it opened as the 1944 Christmas showcase at Radio City Music Hall in New York, and Elizabeth was singled out for special attention. Bosley Crowther's reaction in the New York *Times* was typical: "Mr. Brown has also drawn some excellent performances from his cast, especially from little Elizabeth Taylor, who plays the role of the horse-loving girl. Her face is alive with youthful spirit, her voice has the softness of sweet song and her whole manner in the picture is one of refreshing grace." To this day, Taylor names the film as her favorite.

Left: MGM's mythic ruler, Louis B. Mayer, accepts a ceramic horse from his *National Velvet* star. Relations between the two weren't always so cozy. Eighteen months later, when Sara criticized a script he had in mind for Elizabeth, Mayer reacted crudely. "You and your daughter are nothing, guttersnipes," he shouted. "I can put you back there." Elizabeth was outraged: "Don't you dare to speak to my mother like that. You and your studio can go to hell!" She bolted from his office, refused to go back and apologize, and claims to have never set foot in his office for the duration of Mayer's reign at the studio.

9

A charming study of Elizabeth at thirteen captures the delicate transition between childhood and adolescence.

Above Right: Elizabeth indulges in some tomboy hijinks for the benefit of photographers. Although fame had arrived almost literally overnight, she was handling her newly acquired position with aplomb, and she cooperated willingly with the studio's publicity demands. Her success did, however, necessitate certain changes in her lifestyle.

She was forced to leave the public school she had been happily attending when the principal advised Sara that the other children were too busy "staring at Elizabeth" to concentrate on their studies. She was subsequently enrolled in

MGM's fabled Little Red School House on the studio lot. Although famous for its student roster, the school was depressing for Elizabeth. "I hated (it) because it wasn't *school*...We were required by law to put in three hours a day, so we were doing in that time what normal kids did in six. During a film you'd have a special tutor on the set. So between camera takes you'd cram in ten minutes, twenty minutes of study...going out to act, then being led by the ear back to school and snapping your brain back into being a student."

Opposite: On location in Washington for *Courage of Lassie*, Elizabeth cuddles with Hollywood's premier dog star. The lushly mounted film is really not about Lassie at all. In fact, the collie's name in the picture is Bill, but the studio wisely capitalized on the public's familiarity with the Lassie name for the title.

Elizabeth's love of animals was pointedly mentioned in all publicity releases, but there was nothing phony about her genuine fondness for animals. Her menagerie at the family's new home in Beverly Hills consisted of three dogs, a cat, eight chipmunks (one of whom would soon become famous), a squirrel, and two boarded horses. She once attempted to domesticize a lion cub, until her father put his foot down. *Courage of Lassie* provided Elizabeth with her first top billing and generally good notices. The New York *Daily News* commented, "Elizabeth Taylor is very beautiful and charmingly sincere."

Opposite: The Taylor siblings roast marshmallows for a typical "at home" photo session. This is a rare instance of Howard's participation in his sister's publicity. He was surprisingly unimpressed with her growing fame, and had no desire to follow in her footsteps! Once he defiantly chopped off all of his hair so he wouldn't have to keep an appointment with a studio executive.

Elizabeth, who loves her brother "as much as any man I've ever known," credits Howard with her lifelong aversion to the nickname "Liz." "Like all big brothers, he used to tease me unmercifully," she has said, "calling me Lizzy the Lizzard and Lizzy the Cow. It really got my goat." To this day, no one truly close to Taylor refers to her as "Liz," although she is resigned to use of the nickname in the press, and as a sign of the public's affection.

Left: At the studio, starlet Marie "The Body" McDonald poses with Elizabeth, who holds a copy of her book *Nibbles and Me*, a slim volume

she wrote and illustrated about her favorite pet chipmunk. Because of her celebrity, it was often difficult for Elizabeth to cultivate friends her own age. As a result, she spent many hours at home alone, where she developed a passion for reading and definite art and writing talents. Published in 1946, *Nibbles and Me* has become a prized acquisition for movie memorabilia collectors.

Above: In 1946, MGM "loaned" Elizabeth to Twentieth Century-Fox for the film version of the Broadway comedy *Life With Father*. The movie recounts the adventures of the Day family in turn-of-the-century New York City and placed Elizabeth among a cast that included (seated) Irene Dunne and William Powell, and (standing) Jimmy Lydon, Martin Milner, and ZaSu Pitts. Although confined by the prim costumes and attitudes of the period, Elizabeth began to display a sensual quality on screen for the first time. It was clear that her days as a movie moppet were over.

To kick off the 1946 March of Dimes campaign, Elizabeth participates in a radio broadcast at the White House with Franklin D. Roosevelt, Jr., First Lady Bess Truman and stage actress Cornelia Otis Skinner. Elizabeth and Sara enjoyed their brief sojourn to Washington, D.C., although they were unimpressed with President Harry Truman: "He looks just like Louis B. Mayer," Elizabeth told her mother.

Right: Immediately after completing *Life With Father*, Elizabeth and Jimmy Lydon jitterbugged right into *Cynthia* for MGM. In the title role, Elizabeth played a sickly teenager who defies her overprotective parents (Mary Astor and George Murphy) to gain acceptance among her high-spirited school friends. This homey comedy-drama marked the beginning of Elizabeth's emergence as America's Teen Queen. Of course, she probably lived the most atypical teenage lifestyle imaginable, but after *Cynthia*,

millions of teenagers around the country became loyal fans who identified with Elizabeth in spite of her fabulous beauty, fame and career.

Opposite: At fifteen, Elizabeth poses for her first "cheesecake" photos. The often-remarked-upon maturity of her facial features was now complemented by a rapidly-ripening figure. In just three years, the little girl who had successfully disguised herself as a boy in *National Velvet* had become a sweater girl of admirable proportions. But for all of the attention paid to her as a lovely young star, she was basically lonely. Her status alienated prospective suitors, and the friends her brother brought home often regarded her as a freak, "Howard Taylor's kid sister who is in films."

She was luckier professionally: she had managed to avoid the difficult transitory phase that all other child actresses had gone through. She grew from child to teenager to ingenue with ease and grace.

Top Opposite: With *Cynthia* and *Life With Father*, both released in the summer of 1947, Elizabeth's fan mail reached new heights. *Cynthia*, especially, had a strong appeal, and it brought her the greatest public response she had experienced since *National Velvet*.

Bottom Opposite: Elizabeth's first boyfriend, actor Marshall Thompson, serenades her at the Taylors' Malibu beach house. Thompson (also an MGM player) began dating Elizabeth after they attended the premiere of his film *The Yearling*. The press had a field day covering every angle of her first official "date," but nothing more than a friendly, pleasant relationship ever developed. Thompson is credited, however, with giving Elizabeth her first off-screen kiss.

Playing the first of her spoiled-rich-girl roles in *A Date With Judy*, Elizabeth vamps Robert Stack away from Jane Powell. The film was a frothy blend of adolescent angst, marital mixups and specialty musical numbers. Elizabeth herself sang a brief aria, with her high notes dubbed by a studio singer. If teenagers loved and identified with Elizabeth as *Cynthia*, they now looked upon her with envy and awe. As Carol Pringle, she fairly oozes sex appeal and a surface sophistication that belies her sixteen years.

Much publicity was generated when Elizabeth received her first screen kiss from Stack, and Robert Surtees' color photography highlighted Elizabeth's beauty as never before. Her newly acquired seductive qualities were not lost on the critics when *A Date With Judy* opened in 1948. Reviewer Archer Winsten enthused, "And every time one of the characters refers to her beauty, the spectator echoes the thought. Obviously the proper way to enjoy (the film) is to forget everything but Miss Taylor."

Elizabeth makes up prior to filming a scene for *Julia Misbehaves*, her second 1948 release. She was cast as the romantically confused daughter of Greer Garson and Walter Pidgeon. For Elizabeth, the film's main attraction was the chance to play love scenes opposite the studio's handsome young English import, Peter Lawford. "Peter to me was the last word in sophistication," she said. "He was terribly handsome. The whole company knew I had a crush on him. In the scene where he had to kiss me I was supposed to say, 'Oh Ritchie, what are we going to do?' After the kiss I looked at him and said 'Oh Peter, what am I going to do?' And the whole company fell down laughing." All reports indicate that Elizabeth's infatuation with Lawford never went any further than the soundstage. A romance with the twenty-five-year-old actor would have never been allowed by the ever-watchful Sara.

Julia Misbehaves was not received with enthusiasm by the public, and while her performance was praised by some reviewers, Elizabeth's appearance drew criticism for the first time. *Time* said, "Elizabeth Taylor, who is just beginning to move into grown-up roles, is one of the loveliest girls in movies; but here she is made-up and hair-done and directed into tired, tiresome prettiness." It was true. In its haste to give Taylor a more mature image, MGM had obscured her youthful radiance with cosmetic excess.

Opposite: A refreshing portrait free of the manufactured glamour of the studio's grooming departments. By this time, Elizabeth's crush on Peter Lawford was obsolete. She had begun dating Glenn Davis, a highly-publicized West Point football star, whom she had met at a barbeque at her beach house. They saw each other during the filming of Elizabeth's next film, *Little Women*, and after a few months she coyly told the press that they were "engaged to be engaged."

Bottom Right: Visitors Frank Sinatra and Gene Kelly ham it up with Elizabeth on the *Little Women* set. In a blond wig and bleached eyebrows, she was cast as the self-centered Amy, joining her other "sisters" June Allyson, Janet Leigh, and Margaret O'Brien in the Louisa May Alcott classic about the travails of the March family. For the second time, Elizabeth's mother was played by Mary Astor, who in her autobiography remembers Taylor as professional and excellent in her portrayal, but "faintly smug and superior."

Little Women opened in 1949 at Radio City Music Hall, and proved to be MGM family entertainment at its most sentimental. June Allyson got the most attention for her fine performance as Jo, while Elizabeth received good, though brief, mention.

Right: Little Women brought Peter Lawford and Elizabeth together again, but she was too involved with Glenn Davis to rekindle her interest in Lawford. Instead of a love affair, the two opted for a deep friendship which has lasted for decades. Elizabeth was in good humor during *Little Women* filming, thanks to Davis. When he was shipped to Korea for active duty, she proudly wore his gold football pendant during his seven-month tour.

Opposite: Two months after completing *Little Women,* Elizabeth poses elegantly in London, where she began filming her first adult role as the young wife of thirty-eight-year-old Robert Taylor in *Conspirator.* She was accompanied by her mother, and it was a nostalgic return to Elizabeth's home town for both Taylor women. Life had changed drastically in the ten years since Elizabeth's carefree English childhood. She was now MGM's prize debutante, earning $1000 weekly. But she was beginning to feel hemmed in by her home life. "Perhaps for a few years they (her parents) loved me too much. I was too much a part of their lives. They had no lives of their own, especially my mother."

Above: Although costumed to appear years older for her *Conspirator* role, Elizabeth was still only sixteen and subject to California's educational requirements, which necessitated a tutor on the set. She was mortified by the disparity of her on- and off-screen lives: "How can I concentrate on my education, when Robert Taylor keeps sticking his tongue down my throat?" Elizabeth Taylor was suffering from normal "growing pains" —except that, unlike most teenagers, hers were on international display.

Opposite: For all the studio hoopla about Elizabeth's first grown-up role, *Conspirator* turned out to be a flat, murky melodrama about an American girl marrying a member of the British Guards who is revealed as a Communist spy. MGM was unhappy with the picture, and kept it in the vault for over a year before it was released. Fortunately, Elizabeth managed to emerge unscathed when it finally opened in 1950. *Variety* said, "Elizabeth Taylor is given a big opportunity for an emotional and romantic lead, and comes out with flying colors."

Elizabeth and Glenn Davis attend the 1949 Academy Awards ceremony and seem distracted from the Ronald Colemans behind them—and from each other. This is the last time Elizabeth and her "fiance" will appear in public. In a matter of days, their relationship was over, and Davis had returned to Korea. There is little doubt that the romance was serious, but years later, Taylor discounted its importance: "It was so childish—two sweet children. I remember reading the papers at the time, and I thought, My God, they think it's a big hot romance."

Opposite: In Florida, Elizabeth celebrates her seventeenth birthday and meets William Pawley, Jr., the hirsute son of a well-to-do Miami family. Although she was still involved with Glenn Davis at this time, Elizabeth agreed to date Pawley and they were seen together constantly. When Davis returned from Korea, Elizabeth joined him for a few weeks in California, but it was soon obvious that the romance was over, and Pawley stepped in. He was unaware that Elizabeth was receiving overtures from still another suitor, Howard Hughes.

The elusive billionaire was determined, in his short-lived campaign, to win Elizabeth Taylor. He bought expensive paintings from her father's gallery and flew the entire Taylor family to Reno for a weekend fling at his expense. The lady in question, however, was unimpressed and

she happily became engaged to marry Bill Pawley (who ironically bore a resemblance to Hughes). Sara, who had nixed Peter Lawford and felt ambivalent about Glenn Davis, was pleased with her daughter's choice, referring to Pawley as ". . . brilliant, understanding, strong, poised . . . and full of fun." He was also full of demands. He expected Elizabeth to abandon her film career, relocate to Florida and concentrate entirely on being his wife. She gave his proposal serious thought until she received an offer from Paramount Pictures to star in *A Place in the Sun*, director George Stevens' ambitious production of Theodore Dreiser's classic novel, *An American Tragedy*. Realizing that her career was more important to her than she was previously ready to admit, Elizabeth cancelled her second engagement in less than a year.

A rumpled Van Johnson helps Elizabeth choose publicity portraits between scenes of *The Big Hangover*. In the silly romantic comedy, Johnson is allergic to alcohol, and even a taste leads him into embarrassing drunkenness. As his boss' daughter, Elizabeth helps him overcome the condition.

As with *Conspirator*, MGM viewed the finished film with consternation, and it too was relegated to the shelf—leaving *Little Women* as Elizabeth's sole 1949 release.

Opposite: Conrad "Nicky" Hilton, Jr., and Elizabeth snuggle during their whirlwind courtship. They had met in the fall of 1949 at the Paramount commissary, after Nicky had maneuvered an introduction. He had fallen in love with Elizabeth literally at first sight, after seeing her at a nightclub party. Although still smarting from the Davis and Pawley fiascos, Elizabeth was immediately attracted to the handsome playboy son of the famous hotel magnate, Conrad Hilton. On February 20, 1950, the announcement

of the Taylor-Hilton engagement was made by gossip queen Louella Parsons.

Elizabeth admitted later that, thanks to her sheltered, pampered lifestyle, she was dangerously naive about love and marriage, which she considered synonymous. "So I got engaged to Nick Hilton— at barely eighteen. I really did think that being married would be like living in a little white cottage. . .and me in an organdy apron."

Right: Sara attends her daughter's graduation ceremonies in 1949 at University High School in Los Angeles. Elizabeth, of course, had never attended classes at the school, but received her diploma for her years of study with MGM tutors. It was common practice for young stars to be plopped into the ceremonies of a local school for the purpose of handsome photos in cap and gown for publicity releases.

Opposite: A Place in the Sun was in lengthy post-production when Elizabeth returned to MGM to star as Spencer Tracy's daughter in *Father of the Bride*. As directed by Vincente Minnelli, the film became a wry family comedy about the turmoil an impending wedding can inspire. In the title role, Tracy gave his usual seamless performance, and proved to be an inspiration to Elizabeth, who learned much from the veteran actor. Minnelli called the production, "the shortest, sweetest experience I've ever encountered."

The studio was more than satisfied with the comedy, and when Elizabeth announced to the press that she would shortly be marrying Nicky Hilton, the publicity department was overjoyed with the built-in promotion angle of life imitating art.

Above: On May 6, 1950, Elizabeth and Nicky celebrate following their wedding at the church of the Good Shepherd in Beverly Hills. The event was a giant headache for the Beverly Hills Police Department, because of the thousands of spectators and the traffic snarl created by the arrival of more than six hundred guests. The invitees constituted a veritable Who's Who of the film industry. All of Elizabeth's MGM family was there, as well as the large Hilton family contingent. Studio designer Helen Rose created Taylor's $3500 bridal gown, in a style that showed the cleavage Elizabeth wanted

to, but covered it in lace in the interest of decorum. Edith Head designed several traveling outfits for the honeymoon.

The Hilton wedding was unquestionably the biggest of the year in Hollywood, and practically anywhere else. At the height of the festivities, Elizabeth took her mother aside and said, "Oh Mother! Nick and I are one now, for ever and ever." MGM took shrewd advantage of the public interest in the wedding by releasing *Father of the Bride* exactly one month to the day after the event.

Above: Even on her honeymoon, Elizabeth could not escape her status as a movie star: she obligingly posed in Monte Carlo with a group of smitten sailors. The Hiltons had sailed to the south of France aboard the Queen Mary, where they were entertained by the Duke and Duchess of Windsor. Although Nicky had survived the spectacle of his wedding, he had not reconciled himself to the extent of his new wife's fame. She was besieged constantly by autograph hounds and curiosity seekers.

Hilton reacted peevishly to a situation he should have foreseen. He began drinking heavily, verbally abused Elizabeth in public and, most surprisingly, spent several nights gambling until the wee hours—leaving his beautiful young bride alone and confused in their cabin. Things only worsened after the ship docked in Europe.

Opposite: A sultry studio portrait taken shortly after Elizabeth returned from her honeymoon.

After returning to Hollywood, Nicky and Elizabeth attend a costume party, and the imminent failure of their fledgling marriage is apparent. The more affection Elizabeth lavished on her husband, the more withdrawn he became. "The honeymoon in Europe lasted two weeks," Taylor recalled bitterly. "I should say the marriage lasted for two weeks. Then came, yours sincerely, disillusionment—rude and brutal." Elizabeth kept the failure of her marriage a secret for several months, but in December—after a particularly humiliating fight in which Hilton called her "a fucking bore"—she moved out of their Pacific Palisades house and into a friend's home. She was afraid to return to her parents. She felt guilty about the failure of her marriage and she was planning a divorce—the first in her family's history.

Opposite: In January 1951, Elizabeth is comforted after collapsing on the stand during her divorce proceedings in Santa Monica, California. Sara and Francis, of course, were opposed to the divorce and urged Elizabeth to try and work out her marital problems. Their daughter, however, admitted that she had been "a virgin not only physically but mentally" prior to the marriage and that "at the first sign of trouble between Nick and me, I didn't have a clue how to cope with it."

In court, Elizabeth testified that Nicky had ignored her on the honeymoon, "told me to go to hell, and insulted my mother and me in front of friends." The divorce was granted in twenty minutes. Taylor has never revealed the deepest reasons for the collapse of her first marriage. "I could have gone into such a multitude of really horrendous things, but the hurt that had happened was too private." Elizabeth took a small apartment with a studio friend and tried to nurse her bruised pride and romantic ideals (MGM demanded the wedding gown back when the divorce was granted). Years later, she admitted that she was hospitalized for nervous exhaustion, ulcers and colitis during this period, and that it took her months to recover from the emotional ordeal. "When you are young and you fall off your cloud for the first time," she said, "you try and make yourself believe everything is still beautiful."

2
DREAMGIRL
1951 – 1956

The early 1950s was a relatively placid period in Elizabeth Taylor's life. Although she had started the decade shakily with an unhappy first marriage, her growing career helped to restore her confidence, as did important new friends like Montgomery Clift and Edith Head. By 1952, she had been married again—to handsome British actor Michael Wilding, who was twenty years her senior.

Wilding was sophisticated, patient and understanding with his beautiful young wife, and he brought great stability to her lifestyle. He also brought her motherhood. Michael, Jr., was born in 1953, and Christopher in 1955. Elizabeth adored being a mother, and she had no difficulty adjusting to her new role as a homey, Beverly Hills matron.

Of course, she was no ordinary housewife. She was also busy building a highly successful career as an actress. Although the days of the all-powerful studio system were numbered, Taylor was still under the guidance and tutelage of MGM. She was, in fact, one of the few holdovers from the Forties that the studio retained during a sweeping "house cleaning" that took place in the mid-Fifties. Unfortunately, her home studio didn't always use great care in selecting vehicles for Elizabeth. Her potential was often more fully realized on "loan out" to other film companies. It is noteworthy that her two finest films during this time were *A Place in the Sun* (1951), made at Paramount, and *Giant* (1956), for Warner Brothers.

Elizabeth's beauty flourished during this period as well. From film to film she grew lovelier and sexier. Motherhood only served to make her more stunning, and she became an unattainable fantasy for millions of men. At this point, because of her family-oriented personal life, she was well liked by women too. It would be a few years before she became a threat.

By 1956, she was a major star—though not yet in the category of a Brando or Monroe. As her stardom inflated, however, her relationship with Wilding suffered. Only twenty-four, Elizabeth was still learning about life, growing and changing. Wilding was middle-aged, and settled in his ways and attitudes. Their passion had changed to a warm friendship, and they agreed to end the marriage. Late in 1956, Taylor announced their separation—and in so doing opened herself up to new adventures and, most importantly, to a fascinating new man.

During the final months of her marriage to Nicky, Elizabeth was grateful for the distraction of work. "My career gave me something to do," she said. Of course, MGM was happy to oblige. Following the tremendous success of *Father of the Bride*, including an Oscar nomination as Best Picture of 1950, the studio brought the same creative team together for a sequel, *Father's Little Dividend*, in which newlyweds Elizabeth and Don Taylor make grandparents of Spencer Tracy and Joan Bennett.

With chocolate cake, Tracy and Taylor celebrated both the completion of filming and the lasting friendship they had developed. Tracy gave his movie daughter a shoulder to lean on during her marital woes, and for years afterward he would send Elizabeth notes of encouragement at times of crisis in her life.

The reviews for *Father's Little Dividend* were flattering, praising the film as that rarest of achievements, a sequel that complements the original.

Opposite: Immediately following *Dividend*, the studio rushed Elizabeth into a trite comedy, *Love Is Better Than Ever*. She was cast as a small-town dance instructor who falls for a Broadway talent agent (played by Larry Parks).

The most interesting elements of the production were off-screen. The film's young director Stanley Donen was sensitive to Elizabeth's moods and sympathetic to the recent upheaval of her personal life. In turn, she appreciated his talent and his sense of humor. Within a few weeks, Donen and Taylor were involved in a romance—much to the displeasure of Donen's wife. When the film was completed, MGM realized that it was a dog and did not hurry to release it. While it was in limbo, the picture was dealt a deathblow when Larry Parks was called before the House Un-American Activities Committee because of his early Communist sympathies. He fell victim to the rampant McCarthyism of the times and was virtually blacklisted in the film industry. When *Love Is Better Than Ever* was finally released (as the bottom half of a double bill in 1952) it was unanimously panned as a "strained and artificial" romantic comedy.

Above: By the late spring of 1951, Stanley Donen and Elizabeth were dating publicly. The studio objected because of Donen's marital status, but Sara Taylor was just as concerned because he was Jewish. Thriving on the disapproval, Elizabeth employed the romance as a symbol of rebellion and independence—from the studio's dictates, but especially from her mother. Although Donen's wife filed for divorce during this time, a full-fledged scandal never developed. Within a few months, the relationship with Donen was over.

Professionally, 1951 was a diverse year for Elizabeth. Following *Love Is Better Than Ever*, she joined Clark Gable and Esther Williams in walk-on "bits" as themselves in a Howard Keel comedy, *Callaway Went Thataway*. In the summer months she was in England filming *Ivanhoe*, and in August her career took on new luster with the release of the long-awaited *A Place in the Sun*.

Top Right: Director George Stevens was very candid about why he wanted Elizabeth Taylor for the role of Angela Vickers, the archetypical society girl in *A Place in the Sun*: "The part calls for not so much a real girl, as the girl on the candy-box cover, the beautiful girl in the yellow Cadillac convertible that every American boy, sometime or other, thinks he can marry." If Elizabeth was cast primarily as a "living prop," she was unperturbed, and through Stevens' help (and her own intuition) found facets of Angela's character worth exploring. She later reflected, "The first time I considered *acting* when I was young was in *A Place in the Sun*. It was a tricky part, because the girl was so rich and spoiled that it would have been easy to play her as absolutely vacuous. But I think she was a girl who could care a great deal."

Unquestionably, Taylor cared a great deal about her work in this prestigious film project. She was anxious to be taken more seriously as an adult actress, and was thrilled —though apprehensive— about working with Stevens and the highly-regarded, Method-trained actors Montgomery Clift and Shelley Winters.

Bottom Right: From their first meeting, Elizabeth and Montgomery Clift generated an almost palpable electricity. Their unique rapport was im-mediate and lasting. The intense New York actor (whom Brando called "my only competition") had unexpectedly found a soulmate in the pampered Hollywood star. Clift was disarmed by Elizabeth's unyielding honesty and her wicked sense of humor. Unimpressed by her stardom, he called her "Bessie Mae." She in turn was touched by his brooding helplessness and his East Coast sophistication. Together, they shared a mutual disregard for convention, and their liberal use of four-letter words shocked strangers and delighted their friends.

Opposite: A Place in the Sun tells the story of an ambitious young man (Clift) who drowns his pregnant, nagging girlfriend (Winters) in order to pursue a beautiful debutante (Taylor). He is eventually convicted of the crime and executed. Despite the tragic plot, audiences responded eagerly to the film, primarily because of the potent sexual chemistry between Elizabeth and Clift. Stevens framed the couple in sensuous closeups which, combined with urgent, breathy dialogue, conveyed a frank eroticism rare in movies of the time.

A Place in the Sun opened to rave reviews and was immediately acclaimed as one of the great American films of its era. Elizabeth had taken a definite career risk by starring in the stark drama, but she gave a performance of passion and subtlety. The New York *Times* was particularly impressed: "Elizabeth Taylor's delineation of the rich and beauteous Angela is the top effort of her career. It is a shaded, tender performance and one in which her passionate and genuine romance avoids the pathos common to young love as it sometimes comes to the screen."

The film earned multiple Oscar nominations, including Best Picture, but the only major victory was for George Stevens' direction.

On October 8, 1951, President Truman welcomes a contingent of Hollywood notables to the White House in celebration of the 50th anniversary of the American Movie Theatre. The group includes Elizabeth and Paramount kingpin Adolph Zukor in the front row left, Randolph Scott in the upper right corner, and Debbie Reynolds (smiling benignly at Taylor) in the lower right.

Right: Just days later, Elizabeth and Monty congratulate Judy Garland backstage at New York's Palace theatre, where she was in the midst of the first of her famous "comebacks." Taylor and Garland were friends from MGM, and Elizabeth never failed to champion Judy through the years.

Clift and Taylor were a familiar couple around Manhattan during this time, and they loved to talk intimately until dawn in their favorite Italian restaurant. The couple

seriously contemplated marriage. Elizabeth was crazy about Monty, and she was still operating under the theory that if you were in love, you got married. Clift toyed with the idea, primarily because he cared deeply for Taylor and he was going through a phase when he felt that having children might bring some needed stability to his erratic lifestyle and his ambivalent sexual preferences. Instead, Taylor and Clift enjoyed an exceptional friendship, which ultimately outlasted four of Taylor's marriages.

Opposite: A splendid portrait of Elizabeth and Robert Taylor, costars in *Ivanhoe.* Cast as the Jewish, maligned Rebecca in the Sir Walter Scott classic, Elizabeth was delighted to return to England for the location filming—and to rekindle her acquaintance with British matinee idol Michael Wilding, whom she had met two years earlier during *Conspirator* production. Wilding was twenty years older than Taylor, but she convinced him the age difference was unimportant and they began dating regularly.

Six months after completing *Ivanhoe*, and three days prior to her second marriage, Elizabeth poses in New York enroute to London and her husband-to-be, Michael Wilding. She is wearing an enormous sapphire and diamond engagement ring. Taylor had fallen in love with Wilding shortly after they began dating, and proposed marriage to him several times. The suave Britisher, however, was reluctant at the beginning to become deeply involved with a gorgeous American movie star who was young enough to be his daughter. Wilding, in fact, was usually attracted to older women— he was in the process of breaking off an affair with Marlene Dietrich when Taylor began her aggressive courtship.

Opposite: "Elizabeth wants to be married to someone who will love and protect her and that someone, by some heaven-sent luck, turns out to be me," Michael Wilding said to the press following his wedding to Taylor on February 21, 1952 in London. After a brief honeymoon, the couple settled into Wilding's apartment, and allowed photographers to capture this quiet evening.

For a while, Elizabeth contemplated forming an independent production company and staying in England, where Wilding's stardom could remain secure. But MGM wanted her back, and they not only upgraded her contract, but offered one to Wilding as well. By June, the Wildings had relocated to California, where they purchased a home in Bel Air— with money borrowed from the studio.

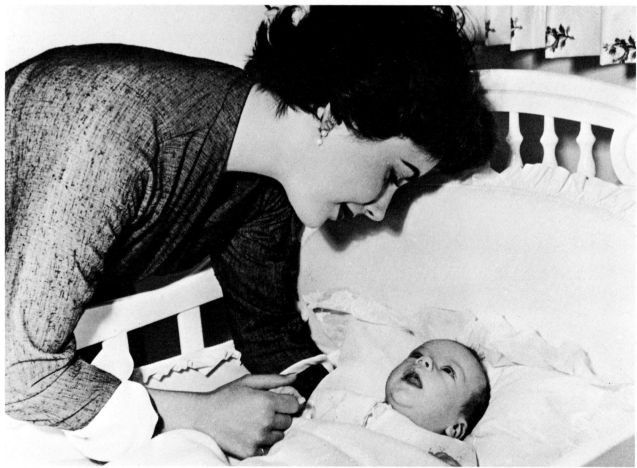

Top Opposite: Returning to work in *The Girl Who Had Everything*, Elizabeth sits on her new husband's lap and enjoys a laugh with costar Fernando Lamas. At just over an hour in length, the film was elevated from the "B" category only by virtue of its cast, which included William Powell as Taylor's father. *The Girl Who Had Everything* was a remake of the 1931 film *A Free Soul* (which propelled Clark Gable to stardom) and concerns a spoiled lawyer's daughter who falls in love with a slick gangster. When it opened in 1953, *Variety* was unimpressed: "Talents of William Powell, Elizabeth Taylor and Fernando Lamas are more or less wasted in the talky, implausible plot, and the dramatics seem dated . . ." Taylor was unconcerned about the film's reception, because its title had proved prophetic: she was pregnant with her first child.

Bottom Opposite: Michael Wilding, Jr., was born on January 6, 1953, and his mother was ecstatic. "I was absolutely idiotic with pride. You would have thought I was the only woman who had ever conceived and carried a child. I was doing (*The Girl Who Had Everything*) until I was five months pregnant, and the baby didn't show at all. I was wearing with ease dresses with twenty-three inches around the waist. But the day I finished the film, I rushed out and bought my maternity wardrobe." Apparently not a moment too soon—Taylor's weight increased by more than forty five pounds while she was carrying.

Motherhood also brought Elizabeth a career dilemma. After recovering from Michael Jr.'s birth, she was put on suspension by MGM for turning down several scripts, and a deal to star in *Roman Holiday* (for which Audrey Hepburn later won an Oscar) fell through. Ironically, Taylor's

next movie came about when Vivien Leigh suffered a nervous breakdown in the jungles of Ceylon, where she was on location for *Elephant Walk*. It was a property originally designed for Elizabeth, which she was forced to turn down several months before because of her pregnancy.

Above: A carefully posed slap characterizes the marital relationship between Taylor and Peter Finch in *Elephant Walk*. As John Wiley, Finch is the essence of male chauvinism—he imports his lovely new bride Ruth from her quiet life in England to his tea plantation in Ceylon, where she is faced with his hedonistic lifestyle and obnoxious drinking buddies.

She must also deal with a suspicious house staff, amorous advances from the plan-

tation's overseer, a cholera epidemic and the elephant stampede that destroys her lavish home and climaxes the movie. Thanks to skillful editing, it was not necessary for Elizabeth to endure these perils in the wilds of Ceylon. All of her scenes were shot in Hollywood, with salvaged location shots of Vivien Leigh, from a distance, spliced into the finished print of the film.

If *Elephant Walk* brought collapse to a troubled Vivien Leigh, it almost turned tragic for Elizabeth Taylor. While posing for this series of publicity photos, a wind-producing machine blew a small metal sliver into Elizabeth's right eye. She recalled, "It had shot deep into the eyeball and had rusted." An ulcerated infection ensued and even after surgery (neces- sitated when her young son accidentally poked her in the eye while playing) there was a two-week period during which doctors despaired of saving the eye. But, as with dozens of illnesses, both minor and catastrophic, dur- ing her lifetime, Taylor astonished everyone by re- covering rapidly and completely.

Opposite: Back on the MGM lot, Elizabeth is determined —despite a hit to her left breast—to win a squirt-gun battle on the set of her new picture, *Rhapsody.*

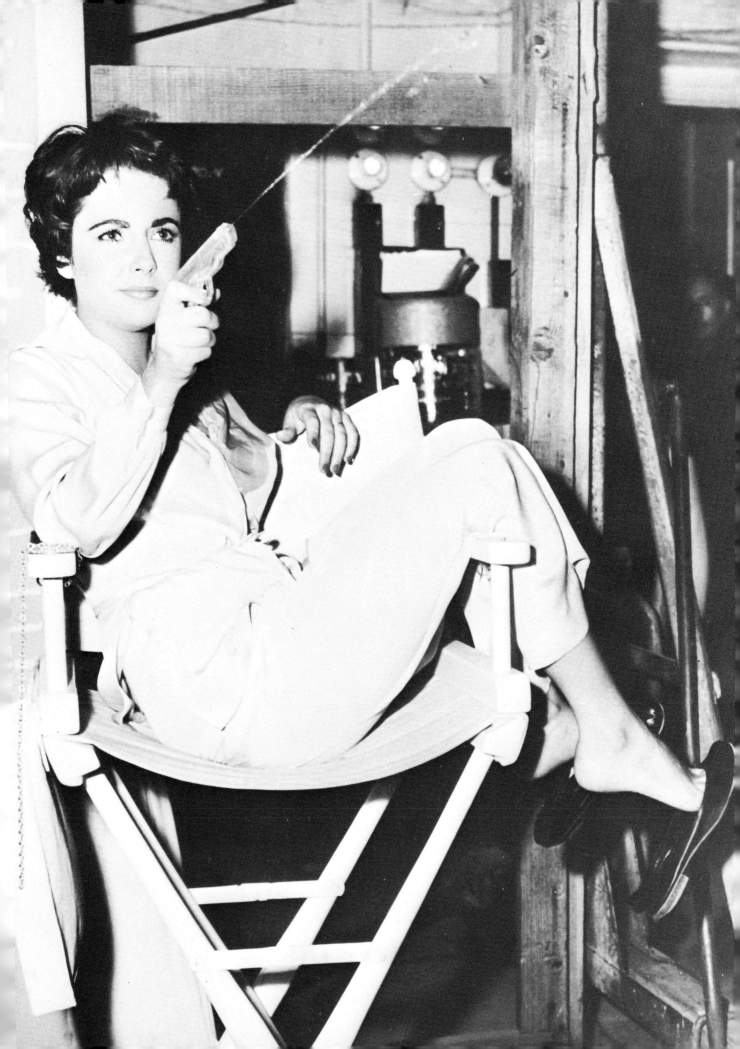

Right: With an expression not unlike those of Marilyn Monroe, Elizabeth reacts to Vittorio Gassman's rather threatening embrace in a portrait from *Rhapsody.* Typical of Taylor's films of the period, *Rhapsody* is a glamorous romantic triangle about a beautiful rich girl in love with a temperamental violinist (Gassman) and an earnest young pianist played by John Ericson. The film offered little acting challenge to the increasingly frustrated Taylor, and was greeted warily by the critics. The New York *Herald Tribune* said, "There is beauty in the picture all right, with Miss Taylor glowing into the camera from every angle... the dramatic pretenses are weak, despite the lofty sentiments and handsome mannikin poses."

Bottom Right: In one of the busiest years of her career, Taylor made three films in 1954; she went directly from *Rhapsody* into the elaborate costume epic, *Beau Brummell.* As Lady Patricia, Elizabeth had little to do except look ravishing in powdered wigs and lend romantic support to the film's title star, Stewart Granger. Never proud of her work in the film, Taylor commented years later, "It was on television and Richard (Burton) turned it on. I had to change the station after about five minutes—I mean, I was so embarrassing in it."

Opposite: Elizabeth feigns terror in a light moment with her costar on the *Beau Brummell* set. She worked easily with Stewart Granger, an off-screen friend. Like Michael Wilding, Granger and his actress wife Jean Simmons were transplanted Britishers who never felt comfortable in Hollywood. With both the Grangers and the Wildings under contract to the same studio, they developed a strong kinship and grew very close. Indeed, during this time gossips intimated that Wilding and Granger had grown close enough to be engaged in a homosexual affair. In his candid autobiography, Granger debunks the story and blames it on gossipist Hedda Hopper—who held a grudge against him.

Bottom Right: In her first death-bed scene since *Jane Eyre*, Elizabeth is comforted by Van Johnson as her guilt-ridden husband in *The Last Time I Saw Paris.* Based on F. Scott Fitzgerald's short story, *Babylon Revisited,* the film became a glossy soap opera under Richard Brooks' direction, although he drew fine performances from his cast. It was this film in fact that inspired Taylor to higher acting aspirations. A decade later she reflected, "*The Last Time I Saw Paris* first convinced me I wanted to be an actress, instead of yawning my way through parts. That girl (Helen, her character in the movie) was off-beat with mercurial flashes of instability —more than just glib dialogue." It was the first time since *A Place in the Sun* that Elizabeth was proud of her work on screen.

Top Right: Sharing a laugh with Monty Clift at the premiere of *The Last Time I Saw Paris,* Taylor was basking in the best reviews of her career. While most critics were unhappy with the film, Elizabeth's work drew praise. *Variety* enthused, "Performancewise, Miss Taylor's work as the heroine should be a milestone for her. It is her best work to date and shows a thorough grasp of the character, which she makes warm and real, not just beautiful." The New York *Herald Tribune* agreed. "She is not only a stunning creature but a vibrant one as she flings herself into the role of an impetuous, alluring, pleasure-loving beauty. . .her performance is such that disillusionment is never out of sight."

Fortunately, Taylor's determination to prove herself as an actress of substance was met with (grudging) support from MGM and the Hollywood establishment. As a result, she was offered better scripts.

Opposite: After adopting the earthy European look so popular in the mid-Fifties, Taylor fusses with her "Italian" hairstyle prior to a photo layout at the Wildings' Hollywood Hills home.

Opposite: The photographer for this session evidently didn't notice the incongruity of posing his subject so sexily in a child's plastic wading pool. This is one of the last times Elizabeth would agree to such typical "girlie" poses. She was about to become a mother for the second time, and her maturing acting talent was elevating her career to new respectability.

Above: The Wilding family welcomes its second son, Christopher, born on February 27, 1955—his mother's twenty-third birthday. The baby's arrival brought his parents' precarious financial situation to a critical state. Although Taylor and Wilding were earning good salaries as movie stars, their expenses were enormous and they were in debt constantly. Because of this, they often had to eschew the lavish lifestyle of their peers. Elizabeth remembered, "I guess our life *had* to be quiet in those years because we were always worrying about going broke. Every time I got pregnant,

kindhearted old MGM would put me on suspension."

Although she spent a lot of time at home, Taylor never developed domestic skills. Visitors often found her home a mess, with her beloved cats and dogs having the run of the house. Michael Wilding admitted to a reporter, "Elizabeth has very little of the housewife in her. She's vague about household things. Forgets to order dinner. . .she never learned to cook and I have no reason to believe she's going to learn now."

Below Right: As newlyweds Leslie and Bick Benedict, Elizabeth and Rock Hudson strike a sultry pose from *Giant*, the epic soap opera based on Edna Ferber's bestseller about a wealthy Texas family's ups and downs in the oil industry. Taylor was thrilled to be cast in this demanding role, which required her to age from a spirited girl of eighteen to a matriarch of fifty.

Casting for *Giant* was complete when the most talked about young actor in Hollywood, James Dean, was signed to play Jett Rink, the rebellious "wildcatter" who is constantly at odds with the powerful Benedict clan.

Above: With physical maturity courtesy of the Warner Bros. make-up department, twenty-two-year-old Elizabeth Taylor was able to play the mother of twenty-one-year-old Carroll Baker in the final portions of the film. By this time, everyone involved with *Giant* was desperate for filming to end. The location work in a stiflingly hot Texas summer was grueling, and George Stevens, who had

shown Taylor such patience and understanding during *A Place in the Sun,* now gave her a hard time about her wardrobe, her elevated star status and her chronic health problems. "I had trouble with my back," Elizabeth explained, "and George was quite convinced it was all psychosomatic. But it is a characteristic of sciatica that it's crippling one moment and disappears the next."

Opposite: In one of the last photographs taken of James Dean, he poses (in aging make-up) with Elizabeth and her son Michael on the *Giant* set. Just days later he was killed in an automobile crash. For all of his moodiness and acting pretensions, Dean charmed his co-workers. Like Montgomery Clift, he brought out Elizabeth's maternal instinct, and although they didn't socialize away from the studio, Dean and Taylor enjoyed a warm friendship.

She was shocked and devastated when he died. "The thing I really remember about *Giant*, the thing I'll never forget, was the night of Jimmy Dean's death . . . I couldn't believe it; none of us could."

A year later, Hudson and Taylor join the immortals by placing their hand and footprints in the forecourt of Hollywood's Chinese Theatre. *Giant* had just opened to excellent reviews and great box office grosses. The film went on to receive ten Oscar nominations, including Best Actor nods for Hudson and Dean, and Best Picture. The only winner proved to be George Stevens for his direction. Although left out of the awards sweepstakes, Taylor received terrific critical praise for her work in the film. The New York *Herald Tribune* enthused, "Elizabeth Taylor's portrayal is compounded of equal parts of fervor and Ferber, and she grows old with a grace and sweetness that can arouse only admiration and envy."

Opposite: A striking study of Taylor at the close of 1956 illustrates the new authority she was beginning to assert as her life was going through a series of important changes. Professionally, she was on the verge of becoming Hollywood's most sought-after actress. The recent attempts to stretch her talent had paid off; she was being offered the best scripts in the business, and her recently-completed performance in the unreleased *Raintree County* was being touted as worthy of an Oscar.

Her personal life was undergoing a dramatic change as well—her marriage to Michael Wilding was ending. There was little bitterness; their relationship had developed into a caring friendship, but to continue the marriage would have been impossible. Taylor said, "It wasn't that we had anything to fight over. We were just not

happy, and I think it was showing in the two boys." The amicable dissolution of the Wilding marriage coincided with the introduction of a significant new man in Elizabeth Taylor's life; a charismatic, brash showman who was known in certain circles as "Todd Almighty."

56

3
TRAGICOMEDY
1957 - 1960

During this short time span, Elizabeth Taylor, who had been living a generally sheltered existence, would experience enough joy and pain to spread over several lifetimes. Her fame grew to tremendous heights, not only because of her movie work, but also because of an amazing series of events in her private life—and the people she shared them with.

In 1957, she was married for the third time—to a man even older than Michael Wilding, but with a youthful, irrepressible spirit. Mike Todd barged through life inspiring either hate or fierce loyalty among the people he touched. Even in the exaggerated show-business world that he inhabited, he was a standout. In work or his personal life, he never beat around the bush. Just days after Elizabeth announced her separation from Wilding, Todd (whom she barely knew) was telling her that she would be his next wife—and shortly, too. As it turned out, he was right. Taylor's life had for years been structured by the studio, and at home by her mature, conservative husband. She was aching for a dramatic change, and Mike Todd obligingly swept her off her feet.

Their greatest joy came when Elizabeth discovered she was pregnant. The joy turned to anguish and worry, however, when their daughter Liza was born dangerously premature. She lay near death for several days and spent her first months in an oxygen tent. Doctors told Taylor that she could never have any more children, and she had to undergo surgery to guarantee against any future pregnancies. Because of the struggle of bringing Liza into the world, she became all the more precious to her parents. Mike, a bragger to begin with, was beside himself with pride. A little over six months later, the happiness of the Todd family was shattered when Mike was killed in a fiery plane crash. Elizabeth went into an epic grief that might have resulted in suicide if she hadn't been sedated and in constant observation by friends and doctors. The public was stunned and sympathetic; Taylor had finally met her perfect match and now he was stolen cruelly from her and their infant daughter.

This attitude would change drastically in less than a year, when Elizabeth fell in love with Todd's best friend Eddie Fisher—who was famously married to Debbie Reynolds. The resulting scandal closed the 1950s with the biggest Hollywood sex story since the decade had begun with the Ingrid Bergman/ Roberto Rossellini affair. Elizabeth was suddenly denounced by church and women's groups, and there was even a brief moment when a move to ban her films was introduced in Congress. Ironically, her movies during this period—*Cat on a Hot Tin Roof, Suddenly, Last Summer* and *Butterfield 8*—were earning a fortune at the box office, and her performances in them garnered her three consecutive Oscar nominations.

Above: Montgomery Clift takes a break from *Raintree County* filming to chat with costar Taylor and Michael Wilding, Jr., a frequent visitor to his mother's movie sets. MGM had taken almost a decade to develop a workable script for *Raintree County*, which they envisioned as a prodigious Civil War saga in the tradition of *Gone With the Wind*. Unfortunately, a plodding storyline and inconsistent performances prevented the film from reaching any level of greatness.

Halfway through filming, Montgomery Clift was almost killed in a grisly automobile accident after a dinner party at Taylor's home. Elizabeth was one of the first on the scene; she cradled Monty's mangled head in her lap while screaming obscenities at press photographers who arrived

before medical help. MGM shut down production on *Raintree County* for over two months while Clift underwent delicate plastic surgery for his extensive facial injuries. His looks were never the same; in the finished film, despite the cameraman's skill, it is obvious which scenes were shot before the accident.

Opposite: In *Raintree County*, Taylor plays Susanna Drake, a New Orleans beauty who seduces Clift, tricks him into marriage, then survives the Civil War, motherhood, and a stay in a mental institution—only to end up drowning in a swamp. Elizabeth brought to the improbable role a multi-layered neurotic quality that earned her fine reviews and her first Oscar nomination as Best Actress.

The quality of her performance is astounding, considering the distractions she was dealing with. She spent many

long nights—after arduous days of filming—trying to pull a pain-wracked, medicated Monty Clift out of a profound depression.

More pleasant, but no less distracting, was a new romance—with an unlikely suitor, Broadway impresario Mike Todd. Brash, confident, and unorthodox, Todd had produced everything from legitimate theater to Sally Rand's fan dance, and had made and lost several fortunes. When he met Taylor, however, he was flush with the success of his motion picture *Around the World in 80 Days*.

Taylor had met Todd only a few times during her marriage to Wilding, but as soon as she announced divorce plans, Todd began a frenzied

campaign to win her. "Don't horse around, you're going to marry me," he told Taylor during one of their first conversations. Elizabeth didn't take him seriously at first, but he sent her expensive gifts daily and ran up a phone bill of epic proportions while she was in Kentucky filming *Raintree County*.

His efforts paid off. Taylor said, "Mike and I really got to know each other on the telephone, talking two or three hours a day." By the time Todd flew Taylor to New York for a two-week break, they were in love and making wedding plans.

Mike Todd and Elizabeth are married in Acapulco on February 2, 1957, while Mexican comic Cantinflas looks on. The wedding took place in Mexico because the Wilding divorce decree was not final, precluding a marriage in the United States. Typically, Todd turned the event into a lavish party. He ordered fifteen thousand flowers, twenty-five cases of champagne, crates of baby lobsters, cracked crabs, and gallons of caviar. The ceremony, however, was relatively simple, with just a few friends in attendance. Todd's longtime friend Eddie Fisher was best man, while Fisher's wife Debbie Reynolds served as Taylor's matron of honor.

The Todd marriage differed little from the courtship; Mike lavished expensive gifts of jewelry on his bride and threw elaborate parties in her honor. He called her "My broad Lizzie Schwartzkopf" and rejoiced in her beauty—which had taken on a new radiance. Taylor, though dumbfounded by Todd's *chutzpah* (and the speed with which he had wooed and won her), was ripe for this highpowered devotion. She grew to love his extravagance, his disregard for subtlety, and the excitement he generated wherever they went. He couldn't have been less like Michael Wilding. Many of Taylor's friends felt that she had finally met her match—a man who was as strong-willed, dramatic and stubborn as she was, and just as much in love with a life of luxury.

Opposite: Attending the Cannes Film Festival, Elizabeth wears a spectacular diamond tiara that was only part of the treasure trove she received from Todd during their European tour to promote *Around the World in 80 Days*. Every time they attended a gala opening for the film, there was a new necklace or earrings or a Paris gown. Years later—in a classic understatement—Taylor commented, "I think he liked to see me in pretty jewelry."

64

The Fishers and the Todds attend the races at Epsom Downs in England. The cementing bond in this curious foursome was Fisher's worshipful devotion to Todd —the two men had been best friends for years. No one was surprised when Eddie and Debbie decided to name their son Todd. A similar friendship never developed between Reynolds and Taylor. They were friendly only because their husbands were inseparable. Although both women were actresses, they had little in common. In his autobiography, Fisher points up the marked contrast between the two: "Elizabeth with her flashy dresses and even flashier jewelry, Debbie in clothes that made her look like everybody's high school sweetheart; Elizabeth with a cigarette in her mouth and a drink in her hand, Debbie giving us all prim lectures on the evils of smoking and drinking. She thought her virtue was her one superiority over Elizabeth, so she played her Girl Scout role to the hilt."

Opposite: One of the most publicized moments in the Todd marriage was this disagreement at the London airport, where they had just missed a plane for Nice. Before a throng of reporters, Mike and Elizabeth engaged in a healthy spat about whose fault it was that they were late. Todd admitted that "for a change, it was my fault." Taylor, enraged at the insinuation that she was chronically tardy, resorted to emphatic hand gestures and grimaces. Within minutes, the situation was settled when Todd chartered a plane, but the incident, thanks to a corps of photographers, made news all over the world.

Top Opposite: Raintree County costar Eva Marie Saint and her husband join the Todds for a party in New York.

Bottom Opposite: Elizabeth Frances Todd is carried home from the Connecticut hospital where she was born on August 6, 1957. Liza, as she was called from the beginning, arrived two months premature and weighed just over four pounds at birth. She hovered near death for several days in an incubator, and spent two months in an oxygen tent. The delivery had been dangerous for mother as well. Taylor's labor was complicated by newly-healed spinal fusion surgery she had undergone months before after a bad fall. Immediately following Liza's birth, doctors insisted on tubular surgery for Elizabeth to insure against future pregnancies. She was tortured by the decision. "It was the worst shock of my life—like being killed."

Above: Liza's remarkable survival, and her mother's courage during the whole ordeal, made Mike Todd doubly proud, and he delighted in boasting to the press: "She looks just like Liz. How's she gonna get along with a handicap like that?" And: ". . . the baby is so beautiful, she makes her mother look like Frankenstein."

Mrs. Todd cuts the first slice of a 17-foot, 1000-pound cake celebrating the first anniversary of the release of *Around the World in 80 Days*. The party, held in Madison Square Garden in October 1957, was the kind of overblown extravaganza that Mike Todd was often criticized for. He invited almost twenty thousand guests, convinced CBS to broadcast the event live, promoted thousands of dollars worth of give-away gifts, and generally encouraged a circus atmosphere that ultimately backfired. Taylor called the evening "an unmitigated disaster."

If the "party" was a flop, no one could deny Todd's right to celebrate; his film had won the Oscar as the Best Picture of 1956 (beating out *Giant*), he was in the best financial position of his career, and he was married to a famous movie star who was now constantly referred to as "the most beautiful woman in the world."

Opposite: Although Mike Todd and Debbie Reynolds also attended the January 1958 Golden Globes ceremonies in Hollywood, it was Fisher and Taylor on stage. Elizabeth is wearing a bizarre "bouffant" evening gown, too much jewelry, and an oddly melancholy expression.

Opposite: The Todds pose happily beside Mike's private plane. Just weeks later, Elizabeth Taylor's life was shattered when the *Lucky Liz* succumbed to turbulence in a storm near Albuquerque during a flight to New York. The crash was sudden and fiery; Mike Todd was killed instantly. Taylor had begged to accompany her husband on the flight, but was persuaded by Todd and her doctor to stay home because of a nagging flu virus and a dangerously high temperature.

As headlines screamed the news of Todd's death, Elizabeth went into a grief of such ferocity that she had to be drugged to prevent any attempts at suicide.

Above: Howard Taylor (right) helps his stunned sister through the Chicago cemetary, where Mike Todd was buried on March 25, 1958. Elizabeth had been flown in from Los Angeles on one of Howard Hughes' private planes. She was under heavy sedation and moved through the ceremonies in a daze. Later, she admitted that she was grateful for her condition because it kept her from completely absorbing the "total horror" of the events around her.

An estimated ten thousand spectators gathered early in the morning to get the best vantage point—as if they were attending a movie premiere. Some munched on potato chips and sat gawking on nearby tombstones, while others swarmed around the mourners trying to get autographs and snapshots. During the services, there were shouts of "Liz, Liz, come on out, Liz!" Later, Taylor's limousine was pummelled by a screaming mob. It was a tragic irony that the kind of carnival atmosphere Mike Todd had promoted so often in life should turn his funeral into an unspeakable nightmare.

When Elizabeth returned to Hollywood, she spent several days in total seclusion. "I couldn't read, I couldn't watch television, I couldn't do anything." Only after she spent some time with her brother and his family at his beach house did she feel strong enough—by mid-April—to return to work on the film she was just beginning when Todd was killed: *Cat on a Hot Tin Roof.*

Opposite: As Maggie the Cat, Taylor contemplates Paul Newman as her sexy, but neglectful, husband Brick in *Cat on a Hot Tin Roof*, the film version of Tennessee Williams' controversial play about the neuroses of an unpleasant southern family. Taylor was thankful to return to work: "I went slightly around the bend with grief. Starting like a robot, I put myself into the world of Maggie the Cat. It was marvelous therapy. I couldn't tolerate what I was, and it gave me somebody else to become."

With support from her co-stars and director Richard Brooks, Elizabeth fulfilled Mike Todd's prophesy that Maggie would represent her finest work to date. The feelings of rage and helplessness she was experiencing surfaced—perhaps subconsciously—in Elizabeth's performance, and she brought Maggie vibrantly to life on screen. Her sex appeal had never been so overt, and her chemistry with Paul Newman was memorable. *Variety's* review was typical: "The frustrations and desires, both as a person and as a woman, the warmth and understanding she molds, the loveliness that is more than a well-turned nose—all these are part of a well-accented, perceptive interpretation." *Cat on a Hot Tin Roof* received six Oscar nominations, including one for Elizabeth as Best Actress. She also received rare praise from Tennessee Williams, who said, "I love Elizabeth. I loved her in *Cat on a Hot Tin Roof*. I think she was the best in the film."

Above: June 1958, Elizabeth makes her first public appearance since Mike Todd's death, visiting Eddie Fisher and Debbie Reynolds backstage at the Tropicana Hotel in Las Vegas following a Fisher nightclub performance. It seemed perfectly natural for Todd's widow to seek out his closest friend for mutual consolation. After Fisher returned to Los Angeles, he began seeing Taylor on a regular basis. They took long drives, and sat for hours talking about Mike and how much they missed him.

Not surprisingly, with Elizabeth so desolate and lonely and Eddie's marriage crumbling, their intimate friendship turned into romance. Fisher remembers it happening with the suddenness of a movie cliché. "Our eyes met and that was it. Not a word was spoken. I was in love with Elizabeth...and I was certain she was in love with me." She was, and by September they were embroiled in the most publicized Hollywood love scandal of the 1950s.

On one of their first "dates," Taylor and Fisher are unable to avoid photographers. One of Hollywood's best-kept secrets was that the Fisher/Reynolds marriage had been in trouble for over a year before Taylor's involvement. Tagged "America's Sweethearts" when they first wed in 1955, Debbie and Eddie realized that they were incompatible after two years, but they stayed together because Debbie discovered she was pregnant with their son Todd,

and because they realized that breaking up might jeopardize their standing as popular entertainers. Also, both of them sincerely did not believe in divorce.

When Fisher and Taylor went public with their affair, the press eagerly cast "Debbie" as the homey wronged wife, "Eddie" as the seducible weakling and "Liz" as the darkly dangerous vamp. By the time the Fishers announced their separation, there were daily headlines about the triangle. Reynolds, in pigtails and gingham, told reporters, "I am deeply shocked by what has happened. We were never happier than we have been in the past year. Eddie is a great guy. Do not blame him for what has happened." The public loved it. Although its collective

heart had gone out to Elizabeth when Todd was killed, there had always been envy mixed with adoration for her, and now the suspicions were confirmed: she was a spoiled Hollywood sexpot who had no qualms about destroying the marriage of one of the decade's cutest couples. Taylor's case was not helped when she tried to defend herself to Hedda Hopper by saying, "Mike's dead and I'm alive." The remark was splashed across every front page in the country, and was the single most damaging element of the entire scandal.

Opposite: On May 12, 1959, Elizabeth Taylor marries Eddie Fisher at the Temple Beth Sholom in Las Vegas, just hours after Fisher had received his final divorce decree from Debbie Reynolds. A few months earlier, Taylor had realized a dream of long standing; she officially embraced Judaism. "It has

nothing to do with any future marriage plans," she told reporters. "This is something I've wanted to do for a long time." She had been studying with famed Los Angeles rabbi Max Nussbaum since her marriage to Mike Todd, whose real name was Avrom Goldbogen. For her conversion, Elizabeth adopted the Hebrew name Elisheba Rachel and began her long devotion to Jewish educational and charitable causes. The Arab nations responded to the news of Taylor's conversion by banning all of her movies. She couldn't have cared less, but was amused four years later when Egyptians were forbidden to see *Cleopatra.*

Opposite: Although they were hounded by the press on their European honeymoon, the Fishers were nonetheless happy to be away from the criticism they were still enduring at home. During the six months prior to their marriage, public pressure had resulted in the cancellation of Fisher's lucrative television series, and Taylor was denied a well-earned Star of the Year award from the theatre owners because "the movie industry is at the mercy of public opinion." Ironically, the same public that disapproved so vehemently of Elizabeth's personal life was making *Cat on a Hot Tin Roof* one of the highest-grossing films of the year.

Above: Fortunately, Eddie's nightclub career did not go the way of his TV series, and his Las Vegas appearances were still highly successful. Some patrons admitted that they attended in the hopes that Elizabeth would be in the audience—which she frequently was. For Fisher's return to the Tropicana, this silly publicity stunt was dreamed up. The humor behind it was indicative of the slowly changing public attitude about Eddie and Elizabeth as a couple. Their marriage certainly helped temper the criticism, as did admissions by Debbie Reynolds that she and Fisher had contemplated separating long before Taylor became the other woman.

79

On location in Spain for *Suddenly, Last Summer*, Fisher talks with his two new stepsons, while Taylor waits for a comb-out. After the critical and commercial success of *Cat on a Hot Tin Roof*, Elizabeth was pleased to be working in another Tennessee Williams vehicle. She knew, however, that it would not be an easy film to make; the story involved homosexuality, madness, greed and cannibalism. In addition she would be acting opposite the formidable Katharine Hepburn and Montgomery Clift, who had deteriorated mentally and physically since their last film together three years earlier.

Taylor trusted director Joseph L. Mankiewicz, and she knew instinctively that her role of Catherine would be the kind of acting showcase she had been fighting for: a mentally confused young woman who must come to terms with ghastly memories surrounding her cousin Sebastian's murder in order to prevent her domineering aunt Violet from allowing her to be lobotomized.

Opposite: Filming *Suddenly, Last Summer* was an unhappy experience for everyone involved, although Taylor didn't much mind the location filming in Spain: she was able to take her family along, and lounge in the sun between scenes. The interiors were shot at Shepperton Studios in London (which had been dressed to resemble Violet Venable's New Orleans home) and the atmosphere was tense from the beginning. Hepburn let it be known immediately that she hated the story they were filming, and she was in constant conflict with Mankiewicz, whom she accused of being too hard on the emotionally battered Monty Clift. Mankiewicz has always denied the charges, claiming that "Elizabeth and I worked desperately to keep Monty going."

Taylor managed to steer clear of much of the turmoil on the set, in order to devote as much time as possible to her demanding role, especially the extended monologue at the end of the film: under the influence of a drug, she must recount the horrors of the previous summer when she witnessed young boys cannibalize her cousin Sebastian. Taylor's riveting performance of this scene, filmed in breathtaking closeups, led Mankiewicz to remark that "she is close to being the greatest actress in the world, and so far she has done it mostly by instinct." The monologue ends with Taylor sobbing uncontrollably, and she admitted years later that she called upon her still potent feelings of grief over the death of Mike Todd to help her with the scene. She received another Oscar nomination for her work in *Suddenly, Last Summer.*

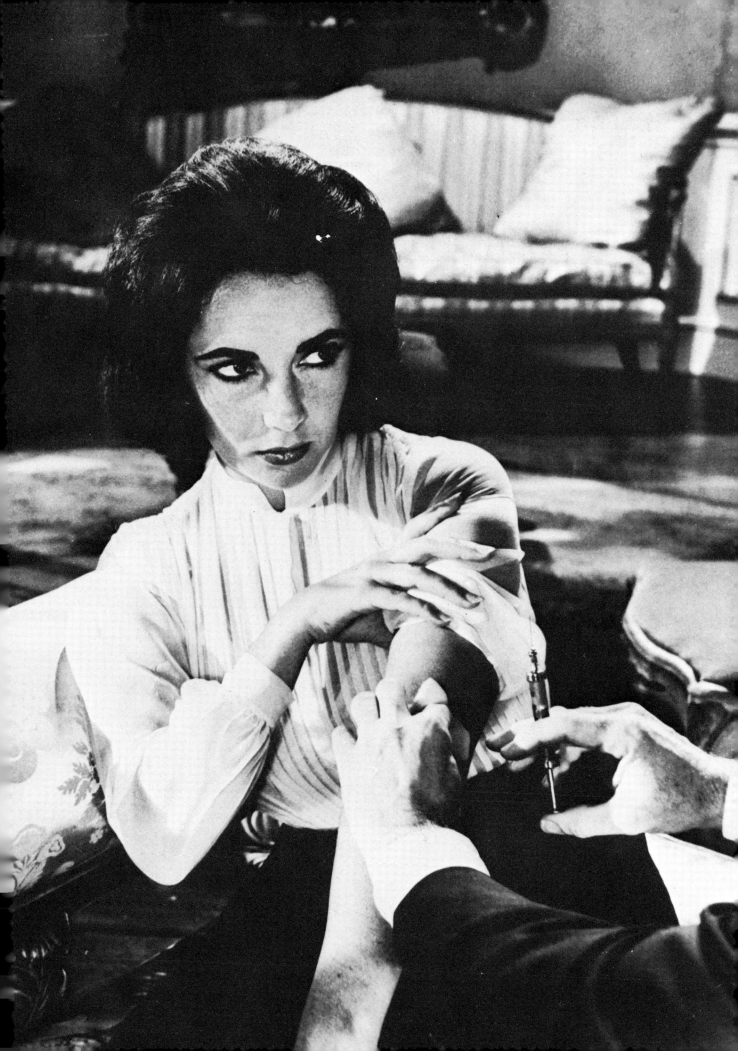

Opposite: Taylor at twenty-eight. Now one of the most famous women in the world, her personal history was already being called legendary.

Taylor is radiant as she attends the Academy Awards ceremony in April 1960. For the third straight year, she did not win the Best Actress Oscar. Although it was commonly agreed that her performance in *Suddenly, Last Summer* could not have been improved upon, the distaste many Academy voters felt for the film's subject matter (mixed with a lingering condemnation of Taylor and Fisher) precluded a victory.

Opposite: As Gloria Wandrous, Elizabeth poses coyly for *Butterfield 8.* Based on a novel by John O'Hara, the film was Taylor's last commitment under her MGM contract, and she eagerly told the press why she had no desire to make the movie: "First, it's the most pornographic script I've ever read, and secondly I don't think the studio is treating me fairly." Although certainly not pornographic, even by 1960 standards, *Butterfield 8* is a sleazy morality tale about a prostitute/model whose disastrous affair with a married man eventually leads to her death.

In light of her recent screen triumphs, Taylor had every reason to turn the project down. But her decision was not based solely on artistic considerations; she had just been offered a fabulous fee to star as *Cleopatra* for Twentieth Century-Fox, and she was anxious to begin filming. MGM, however, held firm. Taylor complied, but made *Butterfield 8* under protest.

Above: On location in New York City, Taylor takes a lunch break from *Butterfield 8* with her husband. Eddie wasn't just visiting the set; he played the supporting role of Steve Carpenter, a Greenwich Village musician who occasionally offered the heroine a platonic shoulder to cry on. Fisher had previously appeared with Debbie Reynolds in the sappy 1956 comedy *Bundle of Joy.* His performance in *Butterfield 8* was sincere but lackluster, and did not result in further movie offers.

Despite her lack of enthusiasm for the picture, and within the limitations of the script, Elizabeth gave an appealing performance in *Butterfield 8*. She was by turns, pragmatic, vulnerable and cynical—longing to be loved, but distrustful of the men she so gladly exploited. *Variety*

praised her: "The picture's major asset is Miss Taylor, who makes what is becoming her annual bid for an Oscar. While the intensity and range of feeling that marked several of her more recent endeavors is slightly reduced in this effort, it is nonetheless a torrid, stinging overall portrayal with one or two brilliantly executed passages within." Taylor was indeed nominated for the fourth consecutive year for a Best Actress Oscar, but she was convinced her performance was unworthy compared to her last few films, and had little hope of winning the award.

Opposite: While Twentieth Century-Fox executives look on, Taylor signs the contract to star in *Cleopatra*. Not since the days of *Gone With the Wind* had so many top actresses been considered for a role. With little regard for historical accuracy, the studio contemplated such box office queens as Audrey Hepburn, Kim Novak, Sophia Loren, Brigitte Bardot, and Marilyn Monroe. Studio president Spyros Skouras was in favor of Irish, red-haired Susan Hayward as the Queen of the Nile. Producer Walter Wanger wanted Taylor, and he submitted *The Life and Times of Cleopatra* for her consideration. Appalled by the quality of the script, yet intrigued at the prospect of playing the part, Elizabeth half-jokingly told the studio, "I'll do it for a million dollars against 10

percent of the gross." To her utter astonishment, they agreed to most of her terms including foreign location filming and drastic script revisions. With the signing of the contract, Elizabeth Taylor became the highest paid performer for a single film in the history of Hollywood, thus ushering in the era of million dollar actors' salaries—much to the chagrin of every studio executive in town.

4
CLEOPATRA
1961 – 1963

One of the most talked-about, expensive motion pictures ever made, *Cleopatra* dominated the lives of its principal characters (and thousands of minor ones) for over three years. There are people who have never seen the film, but who can relate anecdotes about its legendary production. When Elizabeth signed to play the Egyptian Queen, she was still smarting from the hurtful public reaction to her affair with and subsequent marriage to Eddie Fisher.

Shortly after filming on *Cleopatra* began, Taylor won back the collective public sympathy in a drastic fashion, by nearly dying of pneumonia in 1961. After an extended recovery period, during which she won her first Academy Award, she returned to work on *Cleopatra* in Rome. Early in 1962, the improbable happened: she fell madly in love with her Mark Anthony, married Welsh actor Richard Burton. Her second major scandal in four years was underway at full tilt.

This was too much for the public to grasp. They had just rejoiced over her miraculous recovery from a near-fatal illness, they were even warming up to Eddie Fisher again, and now this. Once more, Taylor was decried in the press and from the pulpit, where she was accused of being a threat to the moral standards of civilization. Meanwhile, *Cleopatra* filming continued . . . and continued.

Richard and Elizabeth agonized over their plight. Not wanting to hurt Fisher or Burton's wife of a dozen years, they felt tremendous guilt. They also had to consider the effect their love affair was having on their combined total of five young children. Ultimately, after a great deal of soul-searching and a trial separation, Burton and Taylor realized that they *had* to be together, and damn the consequences.

One of the consequences was a multi-million-dollar lawsuit filed against them by Twentieth Century-Fox for allegedly hurting the potential box office success of *Cleopatra* because of the negative publicity their affair had generated. Of course, when the film opened in 1963, most people went to see it specifically *because* of the notoriety of its stars. The lawsuit, however, took years to settle.

Opposite: Knowing she would be spending long hours in heavy wigs under hot lights while filming *Cleopatra*, Taylor opted for a short hairstyle prior to filming. Pre-production was underway at Pinewood Studios in London, where thousands of dollars worth of sets were being constructed to duplicate the Egypt and Rome of Cleopatra's time. Casting of the other major roles had also been completed; Peter Finch had been signed to portray Julius Caesar, and Mark Anthony would be played by Stephen Boyd.

Above: Following a seven-week illness brought on by tooth problems, Elizabeth makes a rare appearance on the set at Pinewood Studios. By this time, Twentieth Century-Fox was having serious second thoughts about the credibility of shooting an epic, set in the arid sands of Egypt, during a cold English winter. Because of the frigid temperatures, actors supposedly standing in the desert were covered with goosebumps and breathed fog every time they opened their mouths.

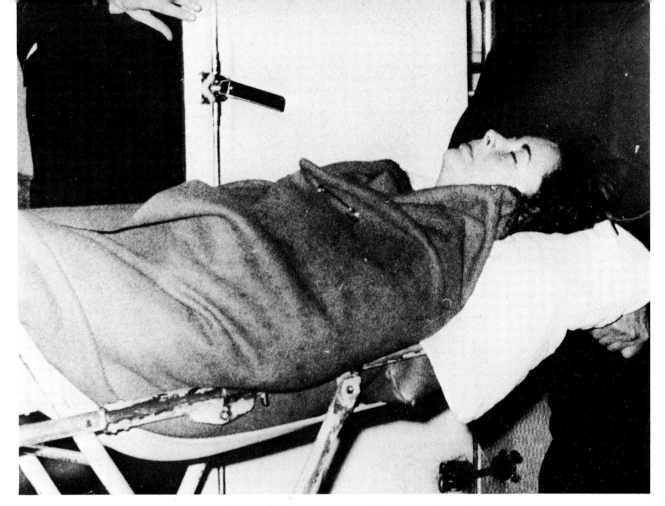

Opposite: During a short break in filming, the Fishers flew to Munich for a seasonal festival, where they enjoyed a carousel ride with Michael and Christopher Wilding. Days later, Eddie was flown back to London for an emergency appendectomy. Taylor was not well herself. She was suffering from a stubborn case of flu, and couldn't shake a nagging cough and a persistent fever.

Above: Two weeks later, on March 4, 1961, Elizabeth (in one of the most famous photographs of the year) is wheeled into the London Clinic. Her lungs were full of fluid, breathing was practically impossible and she was very near death. In her autobiography, Taylor recalls the ensuing events with blunt simplicity: "They got me to the hospital, slit open my throat and stuck a pump down to take this stuff out of my lungs—which if you molded it into a ball and threw it on the floor would bounce. I did come to on the operating table. . . I tried to say the usual bromide, 'Where am I?' But the breath just blew out through the gash in my throat."

The tracheotomy helped her breathing, but she remained desperately ill with advanced pneumonia and a fever that seldom went below 103°. For several days, she hovered near death, and despite a team of local doctors—and the importation of Taylor's private physician from California—her chances of survival were slim. Of course, press representatives from all over the world hovered around the hospital for the latest medical bulletins. Eddie, still recovering from *his* emergency surgery, spent sleepless hours at Elizabeth's bedside and cried with joy when she finally began to rally. She asked for pencil and paper and wrote, "Am I going to die, because I feel like I am." Eddie replied, "No, you're not going to die. Everything's going to be fine." Taylor then wrote, "I love you," and slipped into a deep sleep.

93

Above Left: "I never knew there was so much love in the world," Taylor tells reporters as she and Eddie read get-well messages from all over the world during her recovery. Elizabeth's near-fatal illness had been front-page news everywhere for days. For several hours during the height of the crisis, it was actually reported that she had died.

Overnight, Taylor once again became an object of sympathy, and many of the same people who had condemned her just a year before, now prayed for her recovery. Eddie's tireless devotion during the ordeal had also endeared him to a previously hostile public. With her amazing recuperative powers, Elizabeth regained her health more rapidly than any of her doctors had thought possible. She was tremendously proud of her death-defying recovery, and gave several interviews describing in detail her near-death experiences.

Above Right: The surge of public affection for Elizabeth climaxed when she won the Oscar for her performance in *Butterfield 8.* Still shaky from the illness she had suffered just weeks before, she nevertheless posed happily with Burt Lancaster, who had been named Best Actor for *Elmer Gantry.* While Taylor's performance in *Butterfield 8* had been well received, there was little doubt that she was given the Academy Award for her past achievements—including the bout with pneumonia. She admitted later, "I was filled with profound gratitude at being considered...an actress and not just a movie star. But I knew my performance had not deserved it, that it was a sympathy award."

Opposite: The day after the ceremonies, Taylor poses in her bungalow at the Beverly Hills Hotel. On proud display are several symbolic "awards." The Oscar, of course, validated her hard-earned acting prowess, the wedding band stood for her triumph over the "Debbie" - "Eddie" - "Liz" scandal and—most significantly—the tracheotomy scar was a sign of her greatest victory—over death itself.

Right: As a gag, Elizabeth dons a blond wig and waitress uniform to disrupt an Eddie Fisher performance in Las Vegas. While the Fishers remained in America—at her doctor's suggestion, to insure Taylor's complete recovery—Twentieth Century-Fox was making major decisions about *Cleopatra* in their star's absence. It was decided to shoot the picture in Rome, where the weather would be more acceptable to Taylor, and the necessary pageantry of the film would be cheaper to produce. New casting was also announced. Neither Finch nor Boyd could accommodate the delays in their schedules, so Rex Harrison was signed to play Julius Caesar, and Richard Burton agreed to accept the role of Mark Anthony.

Opposite: Taylor smiles adoringly at Eddie as she sits ringside during his show. To the delight of his audiences, Fisher always sang "That Face" directly and tenderly to his wife. In spite of her recent catastrophic illness, there had been no toll taken on Elizabeth Taylor's celebrated looks: she was more beautiful than ever.

Above: The 1961 Moscow Film Festival was considerably enlivened when Taylor and Gina Lollobrigida showed up wearing identical, supposedly one-of-a-kind Dior gowns. Elizabeth took the highly publicized fashion catastrophe in stride: "I don't think Gina was amused, but I was. Mine is the original." Indeed, Lollobrigida's turned out to be a copy from an Italian dressmaker. It was duly noted in the world press that the actresses had chosen different ways to accessorize their outfits.

Opposite: Back in Rome to resume *Cleopatra* filming, Elizabeth is serenaded romantically by Eddie and local musicians. She was hopeful about the epic she was about to re-start. "If we can capture, in a realistic and human way, the three characters of Cleopatra, Mark Anthony, and Julius Caesar—then we'll have an interesting picture."

Top Opposite: Richard Burton, director Joseph Mankiewicz and Taylor discuss an upcoming scene. This was the first captioned photo sent out over newswires that intimated that Taylor was in the midst of a love affair on *Cleopatra* locations in Rome. The caption disclosed that it was Mankiewicz she was involved with. The director laughed off the rumor with, "Actually, Richard Burton and I are having a fling."

In fact, Taylor had fallen deeply in love with Richard Burton. He had given up his acclaimed role in Broadway's *Camelot* to come aboard the *Cleopatra* barge, and while he was rumored to be a ladies man *par excellence*, his long suffering wife Sybil made sure that he always returned to the nest. Referring to Taylor as "Miss Tits," Burton was not particularly enthusiastic about working in the film. He had starred previously in two historic epics: *The Robe* was successful; *Alexander the Great* had flopped. The last thing he expected was to become involved in a love affair with Elizabeth Taylor that would become historic and alter dozens of lives forever.

Bottom Opposite: Mother's Day, 1962. Taylor has invited her parents to Rome for a short stay; they visit the set and tour the city with Eddie and Elizabeth, and are photographed with their daughter wherever they go. Taylor was happy to see her parents amid the chaos of filming, but she also hoped that the photographs of the family reunion sent to papers everywhere would help rebuff the talk of her affair with Burton.

Above: Taylor and Burton tried at first to be as discreet as possible under the circumstances, but the *paparazzi* would hide out for hours and use telephoto lenses to catch the lovers in as much action as possible. Even sunbathing took on new meaning when it was "Liz" and "Dick."

Their affair was not entered into casually. Though Elizabeth had come to realize that she and Eddie Fisher had no future together, she had no intention of hurting him. At first, Burton, too, had no desire to abandon his solid marriage. And, of course, there were children on both sides to consider. Elizabeth remembers, "There was never any point at which Richard and I began. We just loved each other, and there was no discussion of it. I mean it was there—a fact of our lives."

Opposite: Interesting is the word for the dozens of hairstyles and costumes that Taylor would be wearing in the film. Some, historically accurate, were odd and unflattering; while others seemed too contemporary. In several scenes, her headdress looked authentic, but her gown resembled something worn to a Beverly Hills cocktail party. Gifted designer Irene Sharaff was given instructions by the studio to present Taylor in the most seductive, glamorous fashions—even if they were anachronistic.

Right: Taylor races to the set, trying in vain to avoid photographers. By this time, the affair (or *Le Scandale* as Burton was fond of calling it), had taken over newspaper headlines on a global scale. The public reacted with a combination of scorn and awe; Taylor was taking her movie role as the most famous seductress of all time too seriously, and Burton was helpless to defend himself. Eddie Fisher claims that the public perception of the situation was off-center: "The pursuer (Burton) had become the pursued, and by humiliating her. . .he was trying to keep her in her place. To Elizabeth that meant. . .rejection. No one could treat her that way. *She* had to be the one who did the rejecting. Now she had to have Burton. . .This wasn't a love affair; it was warfare."

HAIR DRESSING DEPT.
PROD. # J-03

ELIZABETH TAYLOR "CLEOPATRA"
Sc. # 219
220

11/16 - 8X10

Above Left: Elizabeth tries to shield her adopted baby Maria from photographers. From the beginning of their marriage, the Fishers (knowing they were unable to have a natural child) wanted to adopt. With the help of actress Maria Schell—for whom she was named—they located a German baby who needed expensive medical help her family was unable to provide. When Taylor first saw the sickly child, she was moved. "She was nine months old, covered with abscesses, suffering from malnutrition, had a crippled hip that was going to cripple her for life—and I just loved her." Ironically, by the time the adoption was fully processed, Eddie Fisher had left Rome and was sheepishly telling reporters that the marriage was over.

Above Right: Liza Todd and Michael Wilding, Jr., visit their mother in Europe, near the completion of *Cleopatra* filming. This was a time of torment for Taylor. She and Richard had decided to try a separation in the hope that they would "get over" one another. She went with her family to Gstaad, Switzerland, and Burton took his wife and children to Geneva. It was at this time that Elizabeth decided, no matter what happened with Burton, that she would divorce Eddie. Her children gave her great consolation during this lonely time. Christopher once told her, "I prayed to God last night that you and Richard would be married." After a few weeks, Taylor and Burton were reunited and decided they had to be together regardless of the havoc their decision would create.

Opposite: *Cleopatra* filming was finally coming to an end. For over three years, Taylor had been involved with a movie that was making history for all the wrong reasons, and she was vastly relieved that it would soon be over. She later said, "It was a little like damnation to everybody. Everything was such a nightmare that it is difficult even to know where to start."

Above: Remaining in England while Burton filmed *Becket*, Elizabeth decided to film her first television special. Aired over CBS in October, 1963, *Elizabeth Taylor in London* was a tour of the city's cultural landmarks conducted by Taylor—who also recited appropriate poetry, as coached by Richard Burton. The show was a ratings success and proved popular with the critics. The Los Angeles *Times* raved, "A sensitive, poetic, warm, delightful hour, beautifully made. . .and a tremendous pleasure to see."

Opposite: A portrait from *The V.I.P.s*, the film Taylor and Burton went into almost immediately following completion of *Cleopatra*. An episodic picture about a group of disparate passengers stranded at the London Airport, *The V.I.P.s* was filmed and released quickly, to capitalize on the storm of publicity surrounding its two stars—who were now living together. In the film, Richard and Elizabeth played Paul and Frances Andros, a wealthy jet-set couple with serious marital woes; Paul has been neglecting his glamorous wife to such a degree that she is secretly planning to run off with her opportunistic lover, played by Louis Jordan. A slick soap opera in the *Grand Hotel* tradition, *The V.I.P.s* was, of course, publicized as a sexy Taylor/Burton vehicle, but it was really more of a showcase for its colorful supporting cast, which included Maggie Smith, Orson Welles, Margaret Rutherford and Rod Taylor.

In the meantime, *Cleopatra* opened in New York in June of 1963, to generally poor reviews. Many critics were surprised to find that Taylor and Burton generated little chemistry on the screen. Most of the acting laurels went to Rex Harrison. *Time* commented, "As for Taylor, she does her dead-level best to portray the *most* woman in world's history. To look at, she is every inch a 'morsel for a monarch.'" One of the few champions of the film was Bosley Crowther, who wrote in the New York *Times,* "One of the great epic films of our day. . .Elizabeth Taylor's Cleopatra is a woman of force and dignity, fired by a fierce ambition to conquer and rule the world." *Cleopatra* did excellent business for several months, but there was no way it could have turned a profit. Final completion costs for the film have never been confirmed by Twentieth Century-Fox, but estimates have gone as high as $60 million.

On location in Puerto Vallarta for *The Night of the Iguana*. When Richard Burton signed to star in the film version of Tennessee Williams' Broadway success, the gossip columnists went on a rampage—this time because Elizabeth Taylor would *not* be costarring. Instead, Burton would be playing opposite a cast the press was sure would produce fireworks: Ava Gardner, Deborah Kerr, and—fresh from *Lolita*—Sue Lyon. The minute Elizabeth and Richard arrived in this small Mexican resort town, the press went into a tizzy. One reporter yelled at Taylor, "Which leading lady do you think Mr. Burton is going to make love to?"

Knowing they would be under constant scrutiny during the time it took to film *Night of the Iguana*, Taylor and Burton tried to avoid any touchy situations with either the cast members or the picture's eccentric director John Huston. Instead they tried to relax and enjoy the natural beauty of the area, and they spent long hours in the local cantina with visiting friends.

Right: A fishing excursion in the Mexican waters off the coast of Puerto Vallarta. Despite the drooling anticipation of the world's press, Burton was involved with no one during *Iguana* filming except Elizabeth. But their intense involvement was proving costly, both financially and emotionally. In order to divorce Eddie Fisher (on the questionable grounds of abandonment and cruel and inhuman treatment), Taylor had to divide their extensive mutual holdings. Burton agonized over the dissolution of his twelve-year marriage to Sybil and how it might affect his beloved daughter Kate. In Puerto Vallarta, he frequently told reporters that he had "no intention" of marrying Taylor. Elizabeth, of course, had no doubt in her mind that they would be married—and as soon as possible.

Opposite: Burton gets a haircut backstage in Toronto where he is about to open in *Hamlet*, March 1964. By now, all obstacles to a Taylor/Burton marriage have been removed. Elizabeth told reporters, "We will be married properly, by a rabbi, in our own dignified good time." Actually, it was just over a week later.

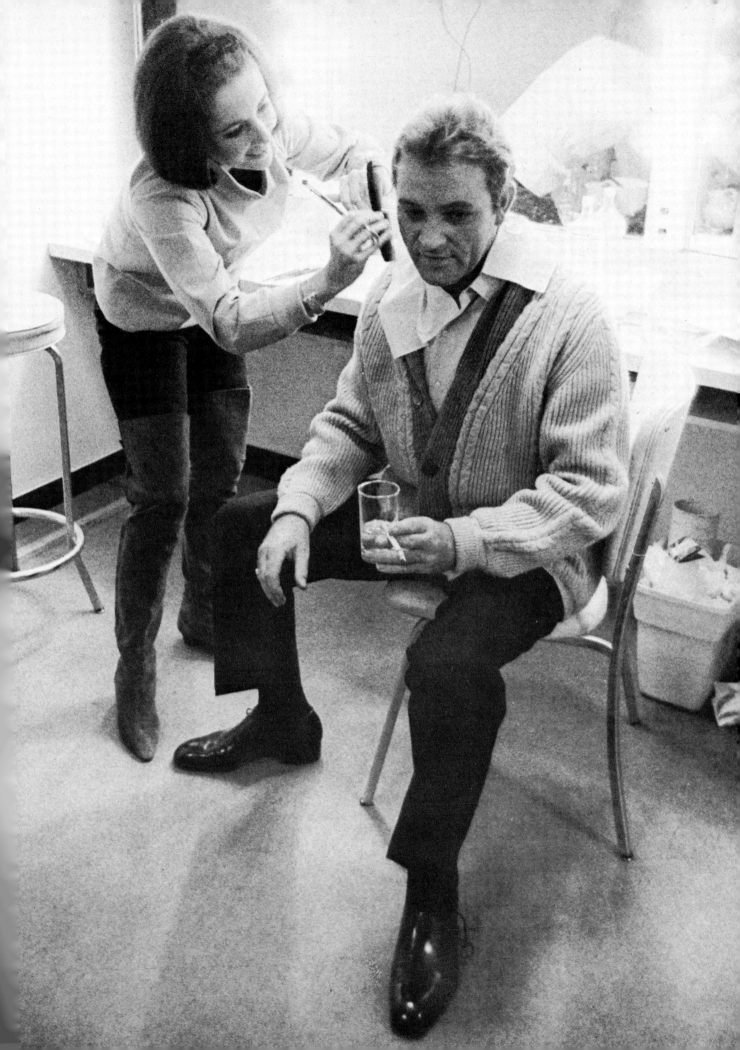

5
THE BURTONS
1 9 6 4 – 1 9 7 3

By the time Richard and Elizabeth married in 1964, they had been living as man and wife for almost two years. The initial outrage their relationship inspired was all but gone. Families had been split apart and convention ignored, but deep down, the public as a whole understood; Burton and Taylor were perfect for each other with a love so great it had survived—even flourished— during the worst of circumstances. They had won out over a scandal that would have completely ruined both of them had it occurred just a few years earlier, in a less liberal time.

With their marriage, they became The Burtons—the most publicized, highly paid and aggrandized acting couple in the world. Even if their special off-screen chemistry didn't crackle with sex appeal on film, it was still exciting and titillating to see them together; whether in potboilers such as *The Sandpiper* (1965) or the following year's classic, *Who's Afraid of Virginia Woolf?*

They hit their absolute peak in 1967. Elizabeth had just won her second Oscar, and Richard had become the most in-demand actor in the business, with or without his wife. The tide turned rapidly, however, in a matter of just three years. The quality of their films deteriorated in direct proportion to the multimillion-dollar salaries they were paid to make them.

By 1970, their magic was wearing thin. Still enormous stars, they were nonetheless slipping at the box office, and the Vietnam War generation resented their excesses. Every few months the papers were reporting that Burton had bought Taylor the world's biggest diamond, or the most expensive fur coat or the longest yacht. As the world entered into a new era of deprivation, the Burtons seemed frivolous and anachronistic.

Their personal relationship suffered as well; there were shouting matches in public about Burton's drinking, and constant rumors about his supposed affairs with other women. Still, it was a shock when they separated and announced divorce plans in 1973.

Opposite: After two years as the world's most notorious and publicized lovers, Richard and Elizabeth become husband and wife on March 15, 1964, in Montreal. "You have gone through great travail in your love for each other," the Unitarian minister said magnanimously at the start of the ceremony. For her fifth wedding, Taylor wore a pale yellow Irene Sharaff gown, and an elaborate hairstyle intertwined with hyacinths. For jewelry, she wore the $150,000 emerald brooch that Burton had given her at the start of their romance.

She was elated following the ceremony. "I'm so happy you can't believe it." Richard confessed, "I have been so nervous about this and having to play *Hamlet* eight times a week that I've lost twelve pounds." The next day, the Burtons returned to Toronto for Richard's evening performance. He received a rousing ovation when, during his final bows, he quoted from the play, "We will have no more marriages."

Above: *Hamlet* moved on to New York and Burton received some of the finest reviews of his career. Each night, after his performance, Elizabeth met him at the theatre and thousands of people gathered to get a glimpse of the world's most famous couple. Taylor reflected on the nightly ritual: "They came, aside from the rubberneckers, I think, partly to pay tribute to Richard as an actor and partly to express friendship. . .a lot of people are beginning to realize that we're not monsters."

Left: When *Night of the Iguana* premiered in New York that summer, Elizabeth was escorted by Montgomery Clift. It was one of the last times they would be seen together at a glamorous show-business function.

Opposite: The Burtons kiss for photographers following their poetry reading at the Lunt-Fontanne theatre on Broadway. The evening, a benefit directed by Richard's foster father and mentor, Phillip Burton, marked Taylor's first stage performance since she had been a tiny girl in England. The audience was delighted with Elizabeth's recitals, especially when she garbled a line from a somber elegy. "I'll begin again," she said calmly. "I got it screwed up."

Above: It was sheer coincidence when the Burtons found themselves booked on the same voyage of the *Queen Elizabeth* with Debbie Reynolds and her second husband, Harry Karl. It was October 1964, five years after the scandal that had enveloped both women, and Eddie Fisher was very definitely a name from the past for both Taylor and Reynolds. Rather than try to ignore each other during the entire trip, the Burtons and the Karls dined together several times and made a point of smiling for photographers.

Above: On the set of their 1965 release *The Sandpiper*, Elizabeth cools off while Richard Burton distractedly holds his script. And no wonder—the screenplay (about an Episcopalian minister's affair with a voluptuous bohemian artist) was trite and hackneyed. It was certainly not the story, nor the chance to work with director Vincente Minnelli, that convinced the Burtons to make *The Sandpiper.* It was the money. Richard and Elizabeth were lavish spenders, and while Burton had made two films since *The V.I.P.s*, Taylor had not. Although the most famous actress in films, she was not easy to insure; her health record, particularly on *Cleopatra*, was not favorable. Consequently, when her old alma mater MGM offered her $1 million to co-star with her husband in *The Sandpiper,* she happily accepted. "We never thought it would be an artistic masterpiece," she explained later.

Opposite: Taylor poses sensuously with a sandpiper. While many critics complimented Elizabeth's earthy, Gypsy-like beauty in the film, the picture itself was roundly disliked. There were particularly harsh words about its voyeuristic angle and the Burtons' willingness to be so crassly exploited. Taylor commented, "A lot of people... may think that *Sandpiper* was written specifically for Richard and me in order to capitalize on our notoriety. Actually, the script had been knocking around for several years, and at first they didn't ask Richard to be in it." Elizabeth's first film in two years proved, in spite of poor reviews, to be a solid moneymaker.

Above: Taylor girlishly rehearses for the most challenging role of her career—that of Martha in the screen version of Edward Albee's explosive play *Who's Afraid of Virginia Woolf?* When she was first approached by producer Ernest Lehman to star in the film, she was flabbergasted: how would audiences accept her playing a frumpy, vulgar, castrating middle-aged shrew? And did she have the acting resources to pull it off? "I never played a part like that," she said. "I couldn't imagine myself as Martha." Fortunately, Richard encouraged her to take the risk and prevent another actress from "creating a sensation" in the role.

During *The Sandpiper* production, Taylor signed for the film, but only after she had convinced Burton to take a career gamble as well by playing George, Martha's browbeaten, caustic, college-professor husband. When producer Lehman proudly announced that he had hired TV and nightclub comic Mike Nichols to direct the Burtons in *Virginia Woolf,* the Hollywood establishment was convinced that the whole project would be a laughable disaster.

Opposite: With the help of thirty extra pounds, padding, a frowsy grey wig and artful make-up, the legendary beauty is transformed into a blowsy harpie. Taylor had to alter not only her looks, but her familiar screen persona as well: "Once I got all the trappings on, Martha just happened without anybody discussing it, without my even thinking much about it." Elizabeth also had to develop a distinctive swagger, and her voice—so often criticized in the past as being too high—had to be deepened to accommodate Martha's gutteral rantings and bawdy laugh. Director Nichols gave his nervous cast the luxury of several weeks of intense rehearsal; Burton was determined to lose any trace of his Welsh accent, and co-stars George Segal and Sandy Dennis needed time to clearly define their odd characters of Nick and Honey, who rounded out this four-character play.

Of course, all the doomsayers were proven wrong when *Who's Afraid of Virginia Woolf?* opened in June 1966 to enormous acclaim—and controversy. Because Warner Bros. had stood firm about the film's salty adult dialogue, there was a great deal of debate about how the picture should be "rated" so that prospective audiences would know what to expect. The studio finally settled for a warning—"No one under eighteen to be admitted unless accompanied by an adult"—which appeared with all of the advertising for the film. It was the first time a major release starring important actors had been so described, and it broke the ground for filmmakers who wished to utilize uncensored dialogue.

If the film was historical, it was also enormously involving and entertaining. The four-member cast was brilliant, but Taylor's performance was a particular revelation. Her Martha is mesmerizing; truculent and gross in the first hour, then vulnerable, exhausted and defeated in the film's final scenes. It isn't a completely flawless performance—there are a few fleeting moments of pure hamminess —but by any standards, Elizabeth's work in *Virginia Woolf* is of towering quality.

The film received rapturous critical notices. *Time* said, "Looking fat and fortyish under a smear of makeup, with her voice pitched well below the belt, Liz as Martha is loud, sexy, vulgar, pungent and yet achieves moments of astonishing tenderness. *Virginia Woolf* at best is a baleful, brutally funny explosion of black humor." *Variety* concurred; "(Taylor's) characterization is at once sensual, spiteful, cynical, pitiable, loathsome, lustful and tender. Shrews. . .always attract initial attention, but the projection of three-dimensional reality requires talent which sustains the interest; the talent is here. Burton delivers a smash portrayal."

Nominated for thirteen Academy Awards, *Virginia Woolf* brought an Oscar to Sandy Dennis for her supporting performance, and Elizabeth won a well-deserved Best Actress award. The film (and its stars) received dozens of other miscellaneous awards and citations from all over the world, and it remains one of the most important pictures of the 1960s. Following completion of the film, the Burtons returned to England where they performed *Doctor Faustus* for a week on stage at Oxford University, to benefit the Oxford Playhouse. Having dropped the weight she had gained for *Virginia Woolf,* Taylor was hailed as a stunning, though mute, Helen of Troy.

Opposite: Elizabeth is caught in a rare pensive moment in *The Taming of the Shrew*. As Katharina in Shakespeare's boisterous comedy, she delivered a robust performance that helped the film become a surprisingly popular success. Taylor admitted to a bit of coaching from her husband and costar, whom she had once called the "Frank Sinatra of Shakespeare." Asked if his wife was comfortable with the language of the play, Burton said, "In *Shrew* she shows definite Shakespearean feeling, the only difficulties being some of the Bard's words that are alien to her. For instance, 'how durst thou' is not common talk in California."

Above: Franco Zeffirelli (left) was the perfect choice to direct *The Taming of the Shrew*. Coming from a background in opera, he brought an earthy pageantry to the proceedings that framed the performances of Burton and Taylor flawlessly. He never allowed their speeches to get "stagey," and he kept the action moving. A beautifully photographed film, *The Taming of the Shrew* drew mixed reviews. Most critics agreed that Burton was letter perfect as Petruchio, but Taylor's performance generated a wide range of reactions. The New York *Journal Tribune* said, "Miss Taylor, for her part, seems to be trying to make up with characterization (let alone squeals) for her discomfort with the language." In contrast, *Saturday Review* was praising. "She has held nothing back in attacking her role with blazing fury, and in her final moments...she is magnificent. I don't know exactly why I felt proud of her, but I did."

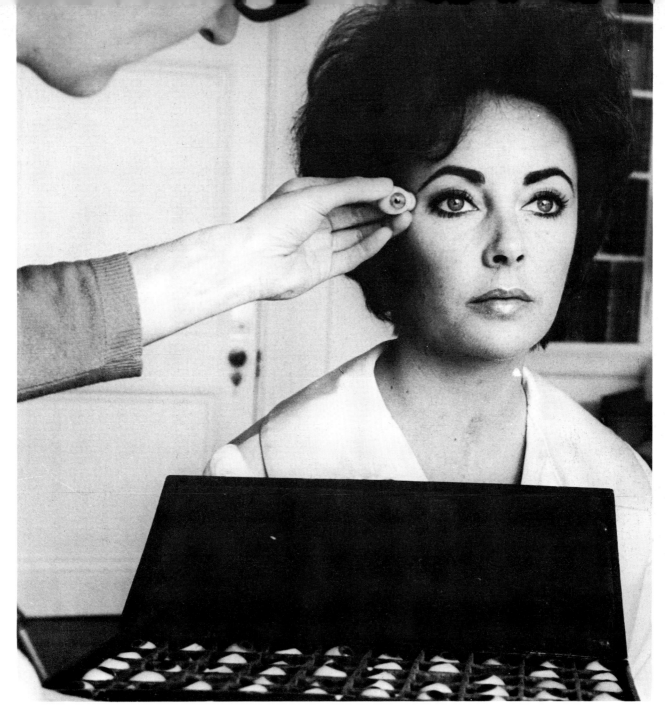

Opposite: The Burtons display their two British Academy Awards and Elizabeth's Oscar for their performances in *Who's Afraid of Virginia Woolf?* By now it seemed eons since the days of *Cleopatra* and the "Liz" and "Dick" scandal. Because their personal notoriety had been matched by acclaimed performances in their last two films, Elizabeth and Richard were now the most celebrated acting couple in the world. Their extravagant lifestyle still drew criticism, but no one could deny their lofty position as superstars. They were at the very pinnacle of their influence and box-office appeal.

Above: Elizabeth sits patiently while a representative from Madame Tussaud's Wax Museum in London tries to match the color of her fabled eyes for a figure the museum is readying for display.

Opposite: A composite of poses of Elizabeth Taylor as Helen of Troy from the poorly received 1967 production of *Doctor Faustus,* starring, produced by, and directed by Richard Burton. As with the stage production of a year earlier, the Burtons donated the proceeds (what few there were) to the Oxford University Players, many of whom were in the movie. Burton raised the money to produce the picture only because *Taming of the Shrew* had been such an unexpected hit. Moviegoers, however, did not respond to the dreary Christopher Marlowe drama as they had the popular Shakespeare classic.

Taylor appeared, wordlessly, in various guises symbolizing the eternal feminine. For one incarnation, she was covered with silver make-up and wore corkscrew aluminum shavings as headgear.

Above: Robert and Ethel Kennedy attend the benefit premiere of *Doctor Faustus* in New York, flanked by Richard and Elizabeth. The screaming mob outside the theatre had nearly prevented the Burtons from entering in time for the screening. The opening was a major event; the film was not: it was thrashed by the critics and disappeared into oblivion.

After Kennedy's murder less than a year later, Taylor paid $50,000 to run a full-page ad in the New York *Times* urging gun control legislation.

Opposite: The implausible climax of Elizabeth's next film, *Reflections in a Golden Eye*: Leonora Penderton (Taylor) is horrified to discover that the young soldier (Robert Forster) who has been sneaking into her room at night to watch her sleep, has just been shot and killed by her husband (Marlon Brando), a repressed homosexual who has been lusting after his victim. Based on a novel by Carson McCullers, *Reflections* became a turgid melodrama on screen. For some reason,

Taylor found the story appealing and agreed to star in the film, provided Monty Clift would be signed to play her husband. She hoped the work would bolster the ailing, depressed Clift, who had not been in a quality movie for some time. Elizabeth even offered to put her salary up as insurance that Clift would complete the picture.

Sadly, Monty died two months before production. Although desolate at having lost one of her dearest friends, Taylor was still committed to the project, and she suggested Marlon Brando—who was also suffering a career slump —to replace Clift. Brando agreed, and casting was completed when Julie Harris and Brian Keith took supporting roles. John Huston agreed to direct the picture in Italy, so Taylor could take advantage of lower income taxes.

Above: With all of the quality talent involved, it is a shame that *Reflections in a Golden Eye* did not emerge as a better film. There are isolated brilliant moments from both Brando and Taylor, but generally all of the film's performances are uncomfortably off-center. Huston's direction is inconsistent, and the decision to film the picture with a nearly monochromatic color scheme was not a wise one. The biggest problem with the film, however, is that audiences simply didn't care a whit about any of the unpleasant characters in the story.

Taylor's Leonora was not a hit with the critics; as written (and acted) she is dominating and emasculating, but without the humor and vulnerability that made Martha in *Virginia Woolf* palatable. Financially, *Reflections* was a flop, and following in the wake of *Doctor Faustus,* the press began to wonder aloud if Elizabeth Taylor was still worth her $1 million plus salary.

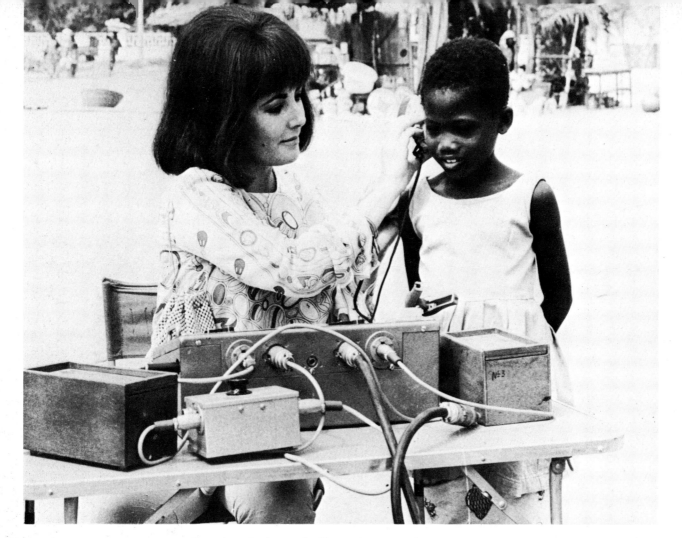

Opposite: In the vaudeville tradition, Taylor carries a card across the stage announcing the next act during a gala Unicef benefit in Paris, late 1967. One can only guess that the theatricality of the evening influenced her choice of apparel.

Above: On location in West Africa for *The Comedians,* Elizabeth demonstrated sound equipment for curious local children. Cast as an afterthought in this Richard Burton vehicle about Haitian political unrest, Taylor played Burton's lover and wife of Peter Ustinov, whom she had worked with in *Beau Brummell.* She had little to do in *The Comedians* except look lovely, make uninhibited love to Burton, and wrestle with a German accent. The film had scenes of strong tension and graphic violence—including a convincing throat-slitting —but at two-and-a-half hours in length, it became ponder-

ous. In spite of some excellent reviews, the picture was a box office dud.

Lillian Gish, who had a supporting role in the film, was surprised to find the Burtons contrary to their image. "They seemed the opposite of everything I had ever read about them," she said. "Elizabeth is a loving, devoted wife and mother. Even the animals preferred her when she came into the room. I told her that I might tell the truth about her, destroy her image, and ruin her career!"

Top Right: In London to celebrate the 1968 re-issue of *Around the World in 80 Days,* Elizabeth dances with Mike Todd, Jr. Two years younger than her stepson, Taylor had grown close to Todd during her brief marriage to his father. They remained friends over the years, and shared a common financial interest in *Around the World in 80 Days.* In 1960, Taylor appeared fleetingly in *Scent of Mystery,* a low-budget chase picture Todd produced to introduce "Smell-O-Vision," a process in which various odors— perfume, shoe polish, etc.— are pumped into the theater during appropriate times on the screen. Neither the film nor Todd's technical innovation found favor with the public.

Bottom Right: The usually camera-shy Howard Taylor visits his sister in Sardinia while she is filming *Boom!* Unexpectedly, he took a bit part, and became one of the few performers in the picture who was not woefully miscast!

Opposite: During a break in filming, Richard and Elizabeth (in a *Boom!* costume) attend a lavish charity gala. By this time, the public had started to turn against the Burtons. Their last few films— separately and together—had not succeeded, and many younger filmgoers found their exaggerated lifestyle and conspicuous consumption vulgar, pretentious and out of step with the times. In the consciousness-raising late 1960s, the Burtons began to seem to many people frivolous and irrelevant.

Opposite: Noel Coward and Taylor relax on the *Boom!* set, 1968. Based on an unsuccessful Tennessee Williams play, the film concerns a fabulously wealthy, terminally ill woman and her quirky relationship with a poet/gigolo who exploits dying matrons. Williams was shocked when the Burtons were cast in his story; Taylor was too young and robust for her role, and Burton too old and authoritative for his. Noel Coward played the Witch of Capri, a part originally written for a woman. Joseph Losey directed the pretentious hodge-podge with flair, and the art direction and photography made *Boom!* an attractive picture to watch, but audiences were not impressed.

Elizabeth narrowly escaped tragedy one day on the Sardinian location, when her lavish dressing room/trailer tumbled over an extremely high cliff and plunged into the ocean. She had left the trailer just moments before. The production also suffered from storm damage to the sets and a fire that threatened several actors.

Above: Also for director Losey in 1968, Taylor made *Secret Ceremony,* in which she costarred with Mia Farrow (pictured) and Robert Mitchum. Certainly one of the strangest films of Elizabeth's career, the plot is so convoluted as to defy concise description. One review said it "unfolds like the anguished hallucination of a schizophrenic mind." Laced with murder, suicide and a touch of lesbianism, *Secret Ceremony* received some excellent reviews, but while initial box office was promising, it was not a commercial hit.

The film made television history when it was first aired in the early Seventies. Universal Studios, in an attempt to clarify the storyline (and clean up some of the sexual implications), filmed new opening and closing sequences in which psychiatrists sit around and explain the goings-on. As a result, the plot became even more confusing to anyone who had never seen the film as originally shown, and Taylor's occupation in the story changed from whore to wig model! *Secret Ceremony* is an unsatisfying picture in either of its forms, but it is worth watching for Elizabeth's fascinating and unique performance.

135

Bottom Right: In Richard Burton's excellent film *Anne of a Thousand Days*, Taylor played an un-billed bit as a masked guest attending an elaborate masquerade ball. Insiders claimed that Elizabeth made a point of being on Burton's set as often as possible because he was supposedly involved romantically with his young leading lady, Genevieve Bujold.

Opposite: Elizabeth shows off the 33.19-carat Krupp diamond that Richard paid over $300,000 for in 1968. Of course, she had been collecting fabulous jewelry for years, but this particular stone became Taylor's prize piece. She adored the admiration it inspired, and paid no attention to claims that it was ostentatious. "I know I'm vulgar," she said, "but would you have me any other way?"

Although she loved gorgeous jewelry, Taylor was often cavalier about the safe-keeping of some of her most expensive gems. She once tossed the Krupp-stone ring to a friend while aboard a yacht, where the enormous diamond could have easily been lost overboard; and during a party following her wedding to Burton, she left another valuable ring sitting on a toilet for several hours where it might have been flushed away.

Top Right: Taylor continues her string of poorly received films with *The Only Game in Town,* opposite Warren Beatty, in 1970. Fresh from his triumph in *Bonnie and Clyde*, Beatty had become a hot property, and there were hopes that he and Taylor would ignite the screen in this comedy-drama about two Las Vegas losers who try to better their lives and fall in love. Even under George Stevens' direction, however, the two stars never created enough of the hoped-for chemistry to make the film entertaining. *The New Yorker* review commented, "After the initial pleasure of finding Elizabeth Taylor looking prettier than she has in years, and watching Warren Beatty's attractively relaxed style, it turns into a sluggish star vehicle of the old, bad days." Although set in Vegas, Taylor insisted the film be shot in Paris where she could be near Burton, who was in the midst of making his own disaster: *Staircase*, a dreadful comedy about two aging homosexual lovers which costarred Rex Harrison.

Opposite: Taylor elicits gasps as she appears on the 1970 Academy Awards telecast to present the Oscar for Best Picture. Deeply tanned and wearing a diaphanous pale blue Edith Head gown, she is also adorned with her latest bauble; the $1.5 million Cartier diamond set in a necklace of flawless smaller diamonds. All smiles on stage, she was deeply disappointed that the Best Actor award had once again eluded Burton, this time for his acclaimed work in *Anne of a Thousand Days.*

Above: Elizabeth makes a rare television appearance as a guest star in the 1970 season opener of *Here's Lucy.* The show was a well-written blend of classic comedy situations: Lucille Ball mistakes Burton for a plumber (he is wearing overalls to elude fans), and eventually she gets Taylor's famous diamond ring stuck on her finger—which leads to a tugging match between the two women. The skit ends hilariously when Ball substitutes her hand—with the ring still stuck—for Elizabeth's during a press reception.

The show came about only because Lucy had bumped into the Burtons at a party and Richard asked her why she hadn't approached them to be in an episode. Ball was delighted to oblige, and the show was a terrific success, earning her the highest ratings of the fall premiere week.

Taylor romps through the 1971 British release, *X, Y and Zee*. Set against the background of London's mod, trendy cafe society, the film is about a traditional romantic triangle—with a twist. Wishy-washy husband Michael Caine is having an affair with lovely Susannah York. His glamorous but shrewish wife (Taylor) finds out about his mistress and not only confronts her, but seduces her as well. It is left up to the audience as to how the situation is resolved. As Zee, Elizabeth had her juiciest role in years, and while she received uniformly good reviews, some critics expressed fear that she was getting locked into variations on her Martha character in *Virginia Woolf*.

Opposite: The Burtons huddle with Peter O'Toole during a 1971 photo session to publicize *Under Milkwood*, a well-made, but scantily distributed film of Dylan Thomas' prose piece originally written for radio dramatization. Taylor played a provincial Welsh prostitute in a cameo role, and was paid only her expenses for her work in the film.

Opposite: "Oh baby, what a grandmother!" wrote the wire services above this July 1971 candid of the Burtons returning from a visit to Elizabeth's first grandchild, Leyla—courtesy of Michael Wilding, Jr., and his wife Beth. When asked by reporters if becoming a granny bothered her, Taylor replied, "You know, everybody assumes that this whole thing would upset me. That's silly. If you want to be honest, I feared turning thirty more than I fear being called Grandma."

Above: February 27, 1972: Taylor turns forty amid an orgy of celebration in Budapest, where Burton is filming *Bluebeard* opposite Raquel Welch (left). Dozens of celebrities, including Princess Grace of Monaco, and Ringo Starr, attended the several days of partying, climaxed when Burton presented Taylor with an exquisite heart-shaped diamond pendant ringed by rubies and emeralds. Valued at $100,000, the piece was over three centuries old and had been fashioned as a love offering for an Indian emperor to give to his wife. Burton admitted to reporters that the cost of throwing his wife's "party"— which included flying guests in from all over the world— had exceeded $72,000.

144

Top Opposite: Beau Bridges as Billy Breedlove and Taylor as Jimmie Jean Jackson in a scene from the Burtons' bizarre 1972 comedy *Hammersmith Is Out.* A satirical variation of the Faust legend, the film cast Burton as a pontificating escapee from an asylum, and Taylor as a malleable waitress with few mental resources. This troubled production was financed independently by a millionaire who had made his fortune in the mobile-home business—a fact reported frequently in the press. After sitting on the shelf for a year, *Hammersmith Is Out* required extensive re-editing before it was considered acceptable for release. It was another box office flop.

Bottom Opposite: The offbeat humor of *Hammersmith Is Out* appealed to several critics and a small minority of film-goers. In a surprise victory, the Burtons won the prestigious David Di Donatello award (Italy's version of the Oscar) for their performances in the film.

Above: In February 1973, the Burtons appear in their first feature made for television, *Divorce: His/Divorce: Hers.* Actually two separate ninety-minute dramas aired on consecutive evenings, the film(s) told of the collapse of a long-term marriage, seen first from the husband's perspective, then his wife's. For a limited theatrical release in Europe, the segments were combined and edited into one picture. The production was a reasonable ratings success, but critics loathed it. *Variety* carped, "Holds all of the joy of standing by at an autopsy." Little fault, however, was found with Taylor's looks. Dressed in a variety of Edith Head fashions, she projected an almost serene loveliness in the film.

Opposite: A tense moment from the 1973 film *Night Watch,* in which Taylor concocts an elaborate scheme to rid herself of her philandering husband, played by Laurence Harvey. Based on a short-lived Broadway play, the film marked Elizabeth's first venture into the mystery-chiller genre; she handled the twists of the plot, and her character's motivations, with expertise. She was pleased to be working with Harvey again; they had remained good friends since their costarring venture in *Butterfield 8.* Taylor was supportive and encouraging during Harvey's bout with terminal cancer, for which he was operated on during the course of filming *Night Watch.*

Above: A distraught Taylor cradles her daughter Maria as their limousine pulls away from New York's Regency Hotel, where moments earlier she had issued an announcement that she and Burton were separating. In the brief statement, written on hotel stationery and passed on to reporters, Taylor said, "I am convinced it would be a good and constructive idea if Richard and I are separated for a while. . .we have been in each other's pockets constantly, never being apart but for matters of life and death, and I believe it has caused a temporary breakdown of communications." She went on to say that she would be relocating to California and concluded the announcement with "Pray for us."

For years, Elizabeth and Richard had been candid about their turbulent relationship. They took sarcastic snipes at each other in public, and in interviews made repeated references to their respective shortcomings: Burton's drinking and wandering eye; Taylor's weight problem and coarse vocabulary. The press dubbed them the "Battling Burtons," but few people thought they would ever really break up. Asked to comment on what looked like the end of an era, Burton said, "You know, when two very volatile people keep hacking away constantly at each other . . .and occasionally engage in a go-of-it with physical force. . .it's bound to happen. I haven't spoken to her since her extraordinary statement. I find the situation wildly fascinating."

147

In the wake of her separation from Burton, Elizabeth starred with Henry Fonda in the elegant 1973 drama *Ash Wednesday*, about an aging Detroit matron who undergoes extensive plastic surgery, including a face and buttocks lift, to try to regain her husband's love. The film generated some controversy because of the graphic depiction of the facial surgery. Through artful editing, director Larry Peerce made audiences squirm as they watched (what looked like) one of the most famous, beautiful faces in the world being sliced, pulled and stitched. Asked if she herself would undergo such surgery, Taylor replied, "not for any man."

Gorgeously photographed on location at a luxurious ski resort in the Italian mountains, *Ash Wednesday* offered many feasts for the eyes, not the least of which was Taylor at her most ravishing. Dressed superbly in Edith Head costumes, she has seldom been lovelier—certainly not in her mature years. Essentially a "woman's picture," the film offered Elizabeth a change of pace; not the least bit screechy or dominating, she conveyed a touching wonder at the restoration of her beauty in the film's early stages and a melancholy resignation at the end when her husband (Fonda) rejects her despite all she has been through to please him. Rex Reed's review of *Ash Wednesday* amounted to a bouquet: "She's subtle, sensitive, glowing with freshness and beauty, fifty pounds lighter in weight; her hair is coiffed simply, her clothes ravishing, her makeup a symphony of perfection. For those who grew up in love with Elizabeth Taylor, this movie is pure magic. She is once again the kind of star marquees light up for." If her private life was in turmoil, at least Taylor could take some solace in this positive career step. *Ash Wednesday* received other good reviews and, while not a blockbuster, it made more money than her last few films had.

6
LEGEND
1974-1984

Elizabeth Taylor did not fully extricate herself romantically from Richard Burton until 1976 (following their divorce, they would re-wed in 1975 and divorce again after a few months), but she knew by 1974 that her life was going in new directions. She scaled down the excessive lifestyle she had lived for a decade, lowered her salary demands for film work and began dating for the first time in almost twenty-five years.

Although she enjoyed a few short relationships with several men, Elizabeth was too marriage-oriented to stay single for long. In 1976 she married a gentleman farmer from Virginia, John Warner, and her life took its most dramatic and unexpected turn. She moved to Virginia, all but gave up her career and settled into a new occupation: political wife.

She eagerly helped Warner campaign for and win a Republican Senate seat from Virginia, even though she had previously voted straight Democratic. Anxious to fit into Washington, D.C., social circles, she was nevertheless something of a glamorous misfit. At public functions, she spoke her mind spontaneously about important issues of the day—even if her opinions were in direct opposition to her husband's. A party girl from way back, she had little concern for the straight-laced image she was expected to adopt as the wife of a conservative Senator.

Most significantly, after the challenge of getting Warner elected, she found herself stuck for weeks at a time on the farm, bored

to death and eating to soothe her frustrations. She would occasionally appear in a film (*A Little Night Music* in 1977), or a television drama (*Return Engagement* in 1978), but it was not enough. The public perceived her in this period as alarmingly overweight and semi-retired. In 1980, she decided to reactivate her career and tackle a new medium, the Broadway stage.

The result was a smashing debut in the classic Lillian Hellman drama *The Little Foxes*. She lost forty pounds for the production, and critics raved about both her performance and her restored beauty. Overnight, she was back in the showbusiness limelight, and she thrived.

With her career in full gear again, there was no way she would be content returning to her quiet Virginia life. She was divorced from John Warner in 1982. She returned to Broadway in 1983, in a much-publicized professional reunion with Richard Burton in Noel Coward's *Private Lives*. Neither the play nor its stars were well received critically, but the fans turned out to see Burton and Taylor together again.

At this writing, Elizabeth has a new man in her life, Victor Luna, a softspoken Mexican lawyer whom she met in the fall of 1982. She has announced that they will wed shortly. Whatever her future holds, Taylor, through her roller coaster of a life, has emerged as a living legend—although she once poohpoohed the title and said, "You're not a legend until you die."

Opposite: Backstage after the 1974 Academy Awards ceremonies, Elizabeth is joined by her son Michael and long-time friend Liza Minnelli. Taylor's appearance on the show received enormous publicity, thanks to a nude man who dashed across the stage just prior to her entrance. The "streaking" fad that was sweeping college campuses had now become a part of Oscar history. A quick-thinking David Niven saved the moment when he thanked the streaker for sharing "his shortcomings" with the worldwide television audience. A flustered Taylor then proceeded to present the Best Picture award to *The Sting*.

A few weeks later, Taylor attended the opening of *That's Entertainment,* a compilation of MGM film clips for which she narrated a segment.

Above: A typically disturbing scene from Taylor's 1974 shocker, *Identikit* (or *The Driver's Seat* as it was called in English-speaking countries). Shown only briefly in America, the Italian production concerns a mentally unbalanced woman who searches frantically for someone to murder her. When it was first shown at the Cannes Film Festival, it elicited shock and confusion from the audience. Only a handful of critics reviewed the picture; among them was Rex Reed, who wrote, "*The Driver's Seat* is a strange, morbid, but intensely fascinating psychological study of a woman going mad that provides Elizabeth Taylor with her most colorful and demanding role in years. She

meets the challenge with imperial efficiency. (She) allows the camera to search out her darting flight into insanity with penetrating self-assurance, giving her most imaginative performance in years." The picture is considered by Taylor buffs to be a regrettably "lost film." It has not reappeared in theatrical distribution, and has never been shown on commercial television.

Above: Almost immediately following her separation from Burton, Elizabeth began seeing businessman Henry Wynberg, whom she had met through Peter Lawford. Wynberg (pictured above with Taylor and her son Christopher) was immediately besieged by the press, which labeled him "a forty-year-old used-car salesman," the latter a reference to one of his businesses in Los Angeles. In late 1973, this new romance was nipped in the bud when Burton flew to Los Angeles to be with Taylor while she recovered from abdominal surgery at UCLA Medical Center. Within days, he had swept Elizabeth out of the hospital—and the country—in a dramatic, highly publicized reconciliation.

After a few months, however, it was clear that the Burtons were more unhappy than ever. The reconciliation attempt was a miserable failure, and on June 6, 1974, Taylor divorced Burton in a courthouse near her vacation home in Gstaad, Switzerland. Wynberg wasted no time in reaffirming his romantic intentions, and in just a few weeks, he and Elizabeth were back in Los Angeles, househunting and talking about marriage.

Opposite: Michael Wilding, Jr., poses reluctantly with his mother as she visits him at the commune where he has been living on and off for several years, October 1975. Relations between Taylor and her children were sometimes strained because of the enormity of her stardom. Michael especially took great pains to avoid the spotlight, and he was, at this time, strongly opposed to Taylor's jet-setting life.

Above: "We are stuck like chicken feathers to tar—for lovely always." So said Elizabeth Taylor after marrying Richard Burton for the second time in October 1975. Henry Wynberg was still seeing Taylor when she reopened communications with Burton by phone in August. Two months later, Wynberg was out and the Burtons were being remarried on the banks of an African river. Elizabeth chose the locale for its romantic simplicity, but she still had to put up with swarms of reporters and photographers.

Following the ceremony, Burton told his bride, "Without you, I was a ghost." Naturally, the remarriage made headlines, and some columnists remarked sarcastically that all was surely well again on Earth, with the Burtons back together. Just months later, however, they had separated again and filed for divorce.

Opposite: Elizabeth spent more than half of 1975 filming *The Bluebird* in Russia. It was a rare collaboration between American and Soviet filmmakers, under the guidance of celebrated director George Cukor. Taylor played several roles in this adaption of the classic children's fantasy by Maeterlinck. She was the warm, homespun Mother (pictured), the beautiful Light, who guides the children of the story through their adventures, and—under disfiguring make-up—a cackling witch. She joined a promising cast which included Jane Fonda, Ava Gardner and Cicely Tyson, but *Bluebird* filming turned out to be a nightmare for everyone. The Russian accommodations were primitive, the working conditions were complicated by the language barrier, and there were numerous illnesses among the actors and crew. Elizabeth had to leave production for several weeks and enter a London hospital with severe amoebic dysentery.

Ultimately costing upwards of $15 million, *The Bluebird* finally lumbered into theaters for Easter 1976, and was panned by the critics and ignored by the public. It is a strangely joyless film, with only occasional highlights. Considering the talent involved with the production, it was a severe disappointment.

Top Opposite: Escorted by George Cukor, Taylor attends the 1976 Oscar ceremonies, at which she closed the show by leading the audience in singing "America the Beautiful" in honor of the country's bicentennial. Single again, Elizabeth was dating several men in New York, most notably Ardeshir Zahedi, the former Iranian ambassador.

Bottom Opposite: England's Queen Elizabeth meets Taylor during a bicentennial dinner in Washington, D.C., on July 8, 1976. Elizabeth's escort for the evening was a blind date that had been arranged by a friend. She describes her first impression of her "date" when he called for her at her hotel: "He had his back to me, and all I saw was that marvelous silver hair. I gathered this was my escort, since he was the only one in white tie in the lobby. He turned around. 'Ah, Miss Taylor.' And I thought *Wow!*" The silver-haired gentleman turned out to be John Warner, former Secretary of the Navy and recently head of the American Revolution Bicentennial Administration. He later confessed that meeting Elizabeth for the first time was a "Wow!" for him, too.

Above: Following their wedding on December 4, 1976, Elizabeth and John Warner settled into a quiet life on Warner's large Virginia farm—until they started working together to get John nominated as Virginia's Republican representative in the U.S. Senate. During 1977, they traveled all over the state attending political fundraisers and greeting as many potential voters as possible. After Warner won the nomination in 1978, they stepped up their efforts, and many observers were surprised at Elizabeth's tireless devotion to her husband's campaign. She endured endless luncheons and charity benefits, and once shook so many hands that her fingers had to be taped for several days.

Above: In a London recording studio, composer Stephen Sondheim looks on as Elizabeth performs his song *Send in the Clowns* for the soundtrack of her new film, *A Little Night Music.* A delightful, sophisticated movie based on the Broadway show, *Night Music* gave Taylor not only a role of rare subtlety, but an opportunity to sing on screen for the first time in thirty years. As Desiree, an aging, flamboyant stage actress in turn-of-the-century Vienna, Elizabeth gave an incisive, wry performance that ranks among her best of recent years. Unfortunately, she was considerably overweight, and many critics reviewed her work based on how she looked: "Her appearance is a shock," wrote *New West.* "Couldn't she have been persuaded to spend a few weeks on liquid protein?" *A Little Night Music* received minimal distribution in the United States in 1977, and is another Taylor film that is often difficult to track down.

During one of John Warner's frequent visits to the film's Austrian location, he and Elizabeth announced their engagement, and showed reporters the red-white-and-blue ring Warner had designed for his fiancée, representing the bicentennial.

Above Right: John Warner accompanies his wife as she is honored as the 1977 Woman of the Year by members of Harvard University's Hasty Pudding Club. Later in the year, Elizabeth was fêted on a TV special, *An All-Star Tribute to Elizabeth Taylor,* in which she was serenaded by former costars and praised by Paul Newman and Bob Hope. The proceeds from the evening helped establish a hospital wing in Taylor's name. Also in 1977, Elizabeth appeared briefly in a hastily-produced movie for television, *Victory at Entebbe.*

Opposite: On the Republican campaign trail, Taylor is almost unrecognizable as she attends a stock-car race. At this point, she was now the heaviest she had ever been, and "Liz Taylor Fat Jokes" were becoming a staple of every TV and Vegas comic. She was puzzled (and hurt) by the public's interest in her weight—which she considers her own business. However, for the press she insisted, "It's happy fat. I eat because I'm so happy." John Warner declared that his nicknames for her were "Chicken Fat" and "my little heifer," but added that, "she is prettier inside than she is outside."

Top Opposite: At the Republican State Convention in Richmond, John Warner has just been nominated as a candidate to represent Virginia in the U.S. Senate. It was June 1978 and Taylor was thrilled that her support and efforts had paid off for John.

Of course, cynics noted that Taylor was the *real* reason people turned out at Warner speeches and rallies, and the candidate himself admitted that his wife was a tremendous asset to his candidacy—just by virtue of who she was. Warner lost the Senate race to Richard Obenshain, but in a bizarre twist of fate shortly after the election, Obenshain was killed in a plane crash. There was a hastily-assembled new election, and Warner this time proved victorious. Two weeks prior to voting day, Taylor grabbed the headlines when she almost choked to death on a chicken bone during a Republican dinner-dance. She was hospitalized briefly, and several days later, told a crowd, "I'm still slightly croaky. I guess you know the story. I was pretty hungry. I ate a piece of chicken and the bone fell in love with my throat."

Bottom Opposite: Elizabeth did reactivate her career briefly when she returned to Hollywood to star as an ex-singer/dancer turned college professor in *Return Engagement,* a television drama aired in November 1978. In the story, a young student (Joseph Bottoms) rents a room in Taylor's home and discovers her hidden past as a performer. Delighted, he coaxes her into recounting her experiences and eventually persuades her to perform a duo with him at the school's annual show. Naturally, they are a smash.

Although matronly and dressed as her character required, Elizabeth gave a charming, balanced performance, and her rapport with Bottoms was evident. Her bittersweet reminiscences about her career in show business were poignantly delivered.

Above: With her children Liza, Christopher and Michael, Elizabeth attends the funeral of Michael Wilding in Chichester, England, in July 1979. An epileptic, Wilding had suffered a fatal head injury as a result of a fall in his home. Taylor and her ex-husband had remained close friends since their divorce in 1957, and they had always shared the responsibilities of raising their two sons. Elizabeth's floral tribute for the funeral read, "Dearest Michael, God bless you. I love you, Elizabeth."

Above: Taylor's only 1980 film release was *The Mirror Crack'd,* a colorful Agatha Christie mystery in which Elizabeth is Marina Gregg, an aging film queen whose life is altered dramatically by a fan's casual kiss on the cheek. Although falling a bit short of the best Christie on film, *The Mirror Crack'd* is a stylish, watchable whodunit that benefited greatly from its cast of seasoned professionals. Taylor (who stepped into the role after Natalie Wood decided against it) gave a self-effacing performance, and was right on target during a high-camp bitch fight with costar Kim Novak. The film reunited Elizabeth with her *Giant* costar and dear friend Rock Hudson, who played her understanding husband, and—from *National Velvet* days—Angela Lansbury, who portrayed the elderly detective Miss Marple.

Opposite: A year later, a beaming, newly-slim Taylor poses with her daughter Maria. (Though severely crippled at the time of her adoption, Maria underwent complicated surgery in the mid-Sixties and now shows no trace of her childhood affliction). The occasion was the pre-opening-night party for Taylor's Broadway debut as Regina Giddens in *The Little Foxes.* Through a chance meeting with producer Zev Bufman in Washington several months earlier, Elizabeth decided to tackle the legitimate stage, and with Bufman's encouragement, she lost over forty pounds during a stay at a health resort and went into a rigorous series of rehearsals. Out-of-town performances of *The Little Foxes* had been sell-outs, and Bufman was confident that Taylor's performance had been polished beautifully in anticipation of the New York opening. He told the press, "There is something terribly vivid about Elizabeth. She has everything it takes to be a great stage actress."

Above: Elizabeth made a dazzling Broadway debut when *The Little Foxes* opened to much ballyhoo on May 7, 1981 at the Martin Beck Theatre. Her recent weight loss and the flattering turn-of-the-century costumes and hairstyles resulted in her looking more beautiful than she had in a long time. Her performance as Lillian Hellman's monstrous creation, Regina Giddens, was excellent. She was particularly memorable in the scene in which she lets her husband (played by Tom Aldredge, pictured) die by refusing to get his medication.

Taylor's reviews were, for the most part, wonderful: Frank Rich in the New York *Times* wrote, "She rewards the role of Regina, that malignant Southern bitch-goddess, with a performance that begins gingerly, soon gathers steam and then explodes into a black and thunderous storm that may just knock you out of your seat." *Time* rhapsodized, "In air and bearing, she possesses regal command. Her arrant good looks, particularly those thrush-startled eyes, fix all other eyes upon her. On glimpsing her, Poe might have written his poem 'To Helen,' apostrophizing the most beguiling beauty of the ancient world."

Surrounded by a supporting cast that included Maureen Stapleton, Dennis Christopher and Anthony Zerbe, Elizabeth made the *Little Foxes* revival the hottest ticket in Manhattan, with a standing-room-only policy in effect for practically every performance. Taylor's triumph in this new area was hailed as courageous, and there were no complaints when she received a Tony Award nomination for her performance. The play went on a short tour which included successful engagements in Los Angeles and London.

Opposite: In character as Regina Giddens, Taylor is formidable and forbidding. Her terrific showing in *The Little Foxes* restored her superstardom to a level she had not enjoyed for several years. Since 1976, she had been living the life of a political wife, and while she blended easily into the Washington and Virginia social circles, she remained at heart an actress, and she missed being recognized for her own accomplishments, rather than those of her husband. She could now admit to the press, "I loved it when John and I were campaigning . . . it was an exciting challenge to work for his election. But once he took office, there was little for me to do except attend teas and be presentable. It was so boring. That's why I put so much weight on. I was bored and eating all the time."

Opposite: The opening night party for *The Little Foxes* was held, as Broadway tradition dictates, at Sardi's restaurant. With Taylor now the toast of Manhattan, observers wondered if Senator Warner would be able to handle the renewed emphasis on the showbiz side of his wife's fame, a side that had been repressed during most of their marriage. "I am really encouraging her," Warner told the press. "My wife and I both have important careers."

Above: A week later, on May 12, 1981 Elizabeth greets fellow MGM alumna Lena Horne at another opening night bash; this one was held at the Parker Meridian Hotel and celebrated the debut of Lena Horne's acclaimed one-woman show.

Opposite: The Warners dance at the party following the 1982 Tony Awards presentation. Taylor didn't win, but it hardly mattered; her hilarious performance as a presenter, fracturing the names of several nominees, was the most talked-about highlight of the show. One of her victims was James Nederlander, who was so enchanted with her creative re-working of his name that he changed the name of his Manhattan restaurant to Taylor's version: *Nedelheimers.*

Above: September 3, 1981. Maureen Stapleton and *Little Foxes* producer Zev Bufman join Elizabeth at Les Mouches nightclub in New York, where Taylor has just received the Damon Runyon/Walter Winchell 1981 Humanitarian Award for her long history of contributing both time and money to numerous charitable organizations all over the world.

Above: In the spring of 1982, Elizabeth created a ratings sensation when she guested for several days on the popular soap opera *General Hospital.* She supposedly asked to be on the show because she was such a fan of Tony Geary (left), a regular on the series. As the mysterious Mrs. Considine, Taylor seemed comfortable working in the alien environment of daytime drama, and she looked fabulous in several glamorous outfits.

Opposite: Rumors that Taylor was about to file for divorce from John Warner were fueled when she showed up at several Los Angeles functions with Tony Geary. Refusing to confirm a romance, he told reporters, "Liz is a romantic. She needs a man around her. She prefers to be with a man rather than a woman. She has few female friends." Taylor and Geary continued to see each other, all the while insisting they were just friends. A little over two months later, Elizabeth filed for divorce from Warner, to the surprise of few. Whether Geary had anything to do with her decision is anyone's guess, but insiders had claimed for months that the Warner marriage was doomed. It was generally agreed that the minute Taylor reactivated her career she would have no desire to give up the spotlight to return to a Virginia farm.

Above: A happy group gets together to tape a Bob Hope comedy special in September 1982. Richard Burton had re-entered Taylor's life the previous February when he unexpectedly showed up for her fiftieth birthday celebration in London, where she had taken *The Little Foxes.* Since then, they had both been mute about a possible re-kindling of their legendary relationship.

Opposite: Elizabeth smiles patiently for photographers following an October 1982 press conference in New York at which she announced she was filing a lawsuit against ABC-TV, which was planning "a docudrama" (read fictionalized biography) on Taylor's life story. Claiming the film would be an invasion of privacy, she told reporters, "My career is at stake and I'm angry. I am my own industry —someday I may write an autobiography or I may even do a film autobiography—and their (project) is taking away from my income."

She also questioned the accuracy of the script. "It's fictionalized," she said, "unless these people were under the carpet or under the bed for my fifty years." Several months later, ABC agreed to drop plans for *The Elizabeth Taylor Story,* in which they had planned to cast Christina Ferrare De Lorean.

Above: Late in 1982, another press conference is called to announce the reunion—professionally, at least—of Taylor and Burton. They planned to star on Broadway together in Noel Coward's stinging romantic comedy, *Private Lives.* They commented that Coward himself told them, during the making of *Boom!,* that they reminded him of his characters Elyot and Amanda, and that they should consider doing the play in the future. It was also announced that *Private Lives* would be coproduced by Taylor and Zev Bufman under the auspices of the Elizabeth Company, and would be just one of a series of plays produced by the two under the company banner.

Although both Richard and Elizabeth had been married and divorced since their last reunion, there would be no romantic reconciliation. What they did not announce to the media was that they were both involved with new companions. Burton with Sally Hay, a director's assistant he met on the set of *Wagner,* a mini-series he filmed in Europe, and Taylor with a quiet Mexican lawyer named Victor Luna.

Opposite: Elizabeth tours an Israeli orphanage during her surprise ten-day peace mission to the Middle East during the Christmas 1982 holidays. She was bruised and bandaged as a result of injuries (including torn ligaments) sustained in an automobile accident. When Taylor embarked on her personal diplomatic trip, she explained, "I want to try to create peace between Israel and Jordan." She said she intended to visit heads of state, and was especially anxious to talk with (then) Israeli Prime Minister Menachem Begin.

The trip (arranged by the publisher of a Los Angeles-based Jewish newspaper) raised eyebrows in the State Department, and was immediately labeled "unofficial"—although one spokesman did say, "Who knows, she may do some good." Elizabeth did meet with Begin and the leader of the Christian militia in southern Lebanon. She had to cut her visit short, however, because of "renewed terrorism" and death threats.

Opposite: Three weeks later, Elizabeth looks radiant as she holds still another press reception to announce her upcoming movie for cable television, *Between Friends,* which will cast her opposite Carol Burnett—who is busy taking pictures of the photographers who are shooting Taylor. Asked to describe the characters they will be playing, Elizabeth blurted out, "She's a nympho, and I'm a drunk." A question about how much money she will receive for the film prompted her to reply, "It'll feed my parrot." Shortly afterward, *Between Friends* went into production in Toronto, and was scheduled for a September airing.

Above: The stars of *Private Lives* leave the Lunt-Fontanne Theatre and smile bravely in the face of disastrous reviews and disappointing ticket sales. Touted in ads as "The theatrical event of the year," the play was instead a prolonged agony for almost everyone involved in the production and surely one of Elizabeth Taylor's worst career decisions. The Boston tryouts were sell-outs, but the critical reaction was scathing. The Boston *Globe* called Taylor's performance "perfectly terrible," while Burton was criticized for being "stiff and hammy." Despite a change of directors, the play showed little improvement when it opened in New York in the summer of 1983, and critics unanimously agreed that Elizabeth was miscast. Despite the reviews, people were anxious to see Taylor and Burton together in a show that in

many ways paralleled their personal relationship. Initially, ticket sales were brisk— even though they were the most expensive in Broadway history for a non-musical show. And every night, there were throngs of fans to greet Elizabeth and Richard as they emerged from the theater.

Eventually, though, bad word-of-mouth and several missed days by Taylor slowed ticket sales, and while the play certainly didn't lose money, it was not the bonanza that had been hoped for. Press attention, however, never abated,

and when Richard Burton married Sally Hay during the run, reporters converged on Elizabeth for a reaction. She told them, "I'm thrilled and delighted for both Richard and Sally. I've known all along they would be married and happy together." When Taylor fell ill with a respiratory infection several days later, gossips insisted she was prostrate with depression over Burton's marriage.

Opposite: May 23, 1983. All in white, Elizabeth arrives at the Waldorf-Astoria hotel in Manhattan to be honored as "Woman of the Year" by the Friars Club, a long-standing showbusiness fraternity. At the banquet in her honor, Taylor was saluted and praised by Frank Sinatra, Dinah Shore, Roger Moore, and Brooke Shields, among dozens of others. Rod McKuen recited a poem he had written for the occasion, and Ella Fitzgerald sang. Comment was made about the absence of Richard Burton, until it was learned that he regrettably had to avoid the celebration because he had stopped drinking and the banquet would have been too great a temptation to endure. Taylor was escorted to her tribute by Victor Luna, who admitted to reporters that he and Elizabeth had discussed marriage.

Above: The unflattering publicity Elizabeth received because of *Private Lives* was counter-balanced by the excellent reviews she got for her work opposite Carol Burnett in *Between Friends* when it was aired over the HBO cable television system in September 1983. Even though the script (about the friendship between two emotionally unfulfilled women of a certain age) drew criticism, the performances of the two unlikely costars were well liked. The Los Angeles *Times* commented, "Although Burnett performs efficiently, it is Taylor who gives *Best Friends* its small distinction, playing tipsy/bitchy to the hilt, bringing out the sharp humor in an otherwise pathetic (character)."

Burnett and Taylor enjoyed working together, and struck up an immediate rapport which helped the credibility of the story they were filming. Asked by a writer to give some insight into Taylor's personality, Carol said, "Elizabeth is confident about herself but not at all egotistical. But then, she's been a star since she was twelve, and survivors like her don't think much about their fame."

Top Opposite: On her way to a *Private Lives* matinee, Taylor—surrounded by bodyguards—dashes past admirers in Beverly Hills. West Coast critics were not as harsh with the play, but the "Liz 'n Dick Show"—as the press had tagged it—was not received with great enthusiasm. Ticket sales were sluggish because patrons were unwilling to pay steep prices to see Elizabeth Taylor in person, only to have her miss the performance as she had several times in New York and Chicago. Also, the cast was tired, and lacked the energy and discipline they had shown on Broadway. In the third act, during a breakfast scene, Taylor took to tossing biscuits into the audience, and the relief on her face at the play's close did not escape the audience's attention.

Bottom Opposite: Victor Luna and Elizabeth pose in a Hollywood restaurant in November 1983. Three months earlier, in New York, Taylor announced her engagement to Luna, and immediately the press wanted to know more about this "Mexican Lawyer." It was learned that he met Elizabeth in the fall of 1982 (reportedly at a memorial service for a mutual friend), and although he was used to a quiet life in Guadalajara with his four daughters, he told reporters that he would make important concessions for his "beautiful lady." Though Taylor gave no date for the wedding, she intimated that she and Luna would probably be wed before the end of 1983.

Above: Now in her fourth decade of fame, Taylor is secure in her position as one of the most celebrated beauties of the twentieth century. Her performing career, however, is in low gear. She has not starred in a theatrical release since 1980; the negative critical and financial reaction to *Private Lives* has resulted in the disbanding of the Elizabeth Theatre Group; and, in spite of the success of *Between Friends,* HBO cancelled plans to tape *Private Lives* for television. However, on the plus side, there is talk of Taylor reviving *Sweet Bird of Youth* for the 1984–85 Broadway season.

Asked recently if she ever planned to retire, she replied without hesitation, "Oh yes. I'm still hoping for the picket fence around the little cottage. . . this other (her career) can't go on forever. I've been working since I was twelve." Of course, she has been threatening to retire since 1957, so it is probably safe to assume that Elizabeth will go right on being one of the most popular—and surely most publicized—actresses in the history of show business.

PHOTO CREDITS

ABOUT THE AUTHOR

Christopher Nickens collaborated with James Spada on the best-selling biography, *Streisand: The Woman and the Legend.* His articles and illustrations have appeared in numerous national publications. Recently, he illustrated the memoirs of actress Anne Francis, *Voices From Home,* and for five years he served as editor and co-writer of *Barbra Quarterly.*

A California native, Mr. Nickens attended Cooper Union University in New York, and he now resides in Los Angeles.